BUTTERFLIES OF DELMARVA

Butterflies
of Delmarva

Elton N. Woodbury

Elton N. Woodbury

Published in association with the Delaware
Nature Society, Inc., by

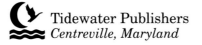
Tidewater Publishers
Centreville, Maryland

Cover illustration by Marcy Dunn Ramsey

Library of Congress Cataloging-in-Publication Data

Woodbury, Elton N.
     Butterflies of Delmarva / Elton N. Woodbury. — 1st ed.
        p.   cm.
     Includes bibliographical references and index.
     ISBN 0-87033-453-0 (pbk.)
     1. Butterflies—Delmarva Peninsula. 2. Butterflies—Delmarva
Peninsula—Identification.   I. Title.
QL551.D45W66   1994
595.78′9′097521—dc20   94-4537

Manufactured in Hong Kong
First edition

In memory of my parents, Dwight A. and
Blanche N. Woodbury, who gave strong support
and encouragement to my interest in butterflies.

CONTENTS

ILLUSTRATIONS AND TABLES

Figures

Plates, following page 58

PAPILIONIDAE:

Pipe-vine Swallowtail (*Battus philenor*)

Zebra Swallowtail (*Eurytides marcellus*)

Tables

PREFACE

I became interested in insects (butterflies in particular) at a very early age. My parents encouraged this entomological interest, but some of my older New England relatives thought it was "wasting my time." My earliest butterfly recollection is of an argument with a neighbor boy also of preschool age. We differed about the reason that butterflies were called butterflies. One of us thought it was because some were mainly butter yellow in color. The other thought that they tasted like butter. Like true scientists, we decided to settle the question by conducting an experiment in which an impartial participant, my friend's much younger sister, would sample a yellow butterfly. The little sister was somewhat reluctant, but after a few lies about how good it would taste, she bit into the bright yellow Clouded Sulphur we provided. The results were immediate: She ran screaming to her mother, who rapidly propelled my friend into the house and called my mother. End of experiment.

My curiosity about butterflies and other insects continued and eventually led to the graduate school of Ohio State University and the receipt of my Ph.D. degree. Before World War II, I was an avid collector, but I later switched to insect photography because I found it more challenging. For the past forty years, I have been photographing Delmarva insects, and, of the sixty-one species of butterflies known to occur in Delmarva, I have photographed all but the very rare King's Hairstreak.

Over the years, I have acquired an appreciation for butterfly gardening, which provides an enjoyable way of observing and learning about butterflies and improves their chances of survival and reproduction as well. These interests have also fostered an understanding of the need for the preservation of the butterflies' natural habitats, especially those of rare and endangered species—and led to this book.

The photographs of adult butterflies included here have been selected to clearly display their identifying features, which are discussed in the species accounts. I hope that the process of identification of butterflies using the photographs and descriptions in *Butterflies of Delmarva* will lead the reader to an interest in the details of their lives and to a knowledge of the requirements necessary for their survival.

ACKNOWLEDGMENTS

The author gratefully acknowledges the many individuals whose help made *Butterflies of Delmarva* possible. C. Eugene and Edna Bennett, Robert B. and Lucile E. duPont Flint, and Mary Fey Jenkins made generous contributions toward the production costs, and Gregory A. Inskip provided legal assistance. The line drawings were contributed by Jane H. Scott.

Volunteers and staff of the Delaware Nature Society provided guidance and inspiration throughout manuscript preparation and publication. I wish to express my thanks to the Board of Directors, especially Bernard S. Dempsey, President; Peter Flint, Director; and Nancy G. Frederick, Vice President and Chair of the Publications Committee; and to the members of the Publications Committee: Henry T. Bush, Franklin C. Daiber, Richard W. Lighty, and Jane H. Scott. Elisabeth B. F. Roszel devoted many hours to editing the text and Yvonne E. Blades to proofreading it.

The idea for this field guide came from Michael E. Riska, Society Executive Director; project supervision and many valuable content suggestions were provided by Lorraine M. Fleming, Manager of Conservation and Preservation; and staff members Donna C. Dorsey, Patricia J. Grimes, Joan W. Priest, and Janice B. Taylor assisted in many ways.

I also must thank Thomas C. Emmel, Ph.D., of the University of Florida, for his very helpful manuscript review and Richard Smith, Jr., of the Maryland Entomological Society, for supplying several published reports on the distribution of Maryland butterflies.

ACKNOWLEDGMENTS

BUTTERFLIES OF DELMARVA

INTRODUCTION

A major purpose of this book is to provide a
reliable and easy means of identifying butterfly
species of the superfamily Papilionoidae that occur
on the Delmarva Peninsula. The region indicated
as the "Delmarva Peninsula" in this publication
consists of the area south of the Pennsylvania state
line, bounded in the west by the Susquehanna
River and the Chesapeake Bay and in the east
by the Delaware River, Delaware Bay, and the
Atlantic Ocean (see figure 1). The total land area
is slightly over 6,000 square miles, comprising all
of the state of Delaware, about one-third of
Maryland, and two counties of Virginia.

Geologically, the Delmarva Peninsula
consists of two distinct regions or physiographic
provinces: the Appalachian Piedmont province
and the Atlantic Coastal Plain province. The
Piedmont is relatively small with a maximum
elevation of 540 feet and is characterized by hills
and valleys with swift-flowing streams. The
Coastal Plain, making up the remainder of the
Delmarva Peninsula, is relatively flat. It has a
maximum elevation of 100 feet with an average
of only 30 feet.

Fig. 1. Delmarva Peninsula.
  Map by Edward G. Tuckmantel.

Because of the difference in elevation between the Piedmont and the Coastal Plain, the boundary between the two is known as the "Fall Line," although Fall "Band" or "Zone" might be more appropriate since in some places it is three or four miles wide. It extends from the extreme northeastern corner of Delaware to the mouth of the Susquehanna River, paralleling the former Baltimore & Ohio Railroad right-of-way.

The flora of the Piedmont (on the north side of the Fall Line) is similar to that of southeastern Pennsylvania, while just below the Fall Line there are many plant species that have reached their northernmost limits. The patterns of regional distribution of Delmarva butterflies are distinctly different from those of plants. For example, northern species of butterflies such as the Compton Tortoise Shell (*Nymphalis vaualbum*), Gray Comma (*Polygonia progne*), and Milbert's Tortoise Shell (*Aglais milberti*) rarely stray south of the Fall Line, but emigrant species such as the Cloudless Sulphur (*Phoebis sennae eubule*), Painted Lady (*Vanessa cardui*), and Buckeye (*Junonia coenia*), from the south, frequently cross over to the Piedmont and beyond.

The first step in identification is to become familiar with the major characteristics of the various families and subfamilies. Size sometimes can be a difficult characteristic to use, since all butterfly species have a degree of variation of dimension related to sexual, seasonal, and climatic differences, but the following information will be helpful as a guide.

All of the butterflies included in this guide are members of the "true butterflies" superfamily Papilionoidae, which is divided into a number of families. Large butterflies (those with a fore-wing length ranging from 2.9 to 7.6 cm) having prominent tails are usually members of the family Papilionidae. The size range of members of the family Danaidae, subfamily Danainae, is similar to that of the Papilionidae family, but the butterflies have no tails. Small- to medium-sized butterflies (having a forewing of 1.5-3.5 cm), which are predominately white, yellow, or bright orange belong to the family Pieridae. Small butterflies (those with forewings of 0.97-2.4 cm), frequently having small threadlike tails, are in the family Lycaenidae; and those with only four normal legs, are either in the family Libytheidae (1.9-2.4 cm), the family Nymphalidae (which has a forewing size ranging widely from 1.4-4.8 cm), the family Apaturidae, subfamily Apaturinae (2.2-3.4 cm), or the family Satyridae, subfamily Satyrinae (1.8-3.2 cm). Table 1, which lists forewing length measurements, is based on *Butterflies East of the Great Plains* by Opler and Krizek.

The next step in identifying a particular species is to leaf through the photographs of the selected family. The species' descriptions in the text will be helpful in distinguishing between "look alike" species such as the Pearl Crescent (*Phyciodes tharos*) and the Silvery Checkerspot (*Charidryas nycteis*).

You can use a net if necessary to capture a butterfly for identification, but handle the insect carefully to avoid injuring it. With wings in the vertical position, grasp the body gently but firmly at the base of the wings and hold between your thumb and forefinger.

Table 1. Butterfly Forewing Length

BUTTERFLY FAMILIES AND SUBGROUPS	SIZE	FOREWING LENGTH IN CENTIMETERS
FAMILY PAPILIONIDAE		
Swallowtails	L	2.9 - 7.6
FAMILY PIERIDAE		
Whites, Orange		
Tips, Sulphurs	S to M	1.5 - 3.5
FAMILY LYCAENIDAE		
Harvesters	S	1.32 - 1.55
Coppers	S	1.2 - 2.2
Hairstreaks	S	1.1 - 2.4
Blues	S	0.97 - 1.52
FAMILY LIBYTHEIDAE		
Snout Butterflies	M	1.9 - 2.4
FAMILY NYMPHALIDAE		
Fritillaries,		
Checkerspots,		
Anglewings,		
Admirals	M	1.4 - 4.8
FAMILY APATURIDAE		
Hackberry Butterflies	M	2.2 - 3.4
FAMILY SATYRIDAE		
Browns, Satyrs,		
Wood Nymphs	M	1.8 - 3.2
FAMILY DANAIDAE		
Monarch	L	4.3 - 5.9
Key: S = Small	M = Medium	L = Large

Members of the superfamily Hesperioidae, family Hesperiidae, commonly known as skippers, are not true butterflies and, therefore, are not included in this guide. Delmarva species of skippers are small, predominantly gray, black, brown, or orange in color, and have a rapid and erratic flight. They can be easily distinguished from members of the Papilionoidae by their antennae which have an elongated, hook-shaped terminal club. A common member of this group is the Silver-spotted Skipper (*Epargyreus clarus*), easily identified by a large white patch on the underside of the hind wing.

Taxonomy and nomenclature of butterfly species in this guide follow *The Common Names of North American Butterflies* (see References).

I. NATURAL HISTORY OF BUTTERFLIES

Taxonomy:
The Place of Butterflies in the Animal Kingdom

An orderly system of classifying and naming organisms was originated in 1758 by Carolus Linnaeus, a Swedish scientist. With minor modifications it has persisted to this day. Latin, then in general use by scientists, was adopted for the names of members of the various categories of kingdom, phylum, class, order, family, genus, and species. Butterflies are placed in the kingdom Animalia, phylum Arthropoda, class Insecta and order Lepidoptera, which includes the true butterflies, skippers, and moths. The scientific name is a Latin binomial made up of the genus and species names. In some cases a subspecies name is added. Thus the scientific name of a species is internationally recognized.

A species may be defined as a group of organisms that possess one or more distinctive characteristics in common and interbreed to produce fertile offspring. Anyone may name a new species, provided that the person follows the rules found in the International Code of Zoological Nomenclature. These rules require publication in a recognized scientific journal, a comparative description of the proposed species, the location of a type specimen, and the definition of a type locality. Priority is also important; the name included with the documentation having the earliest publication date prevails. Scientifically specific names, therefore, provide authentic identities that are accepted and used worldwide.

In addition to the Latinized scientific name, many species have common names that have been established through long usage. The scientific and common names in this book are taken from *The Common Names of North American Butterflies*.

Anatomy

Only those anatomical features that are useful in identification or contribute to an understanding of butterfly life history are included in this section. For a more comprehensive treatment of butterfly anatomy, the reader is referred to *The Butterflies of North America* by James A. Scott (1986).

In common with other insects, butterflies have an outer or exoskeleton which protects and supports the internal organs. A major component and essential constituent of the exoskeleton is a polymerized glucosamine called chitin. The physical properties of chitin can be modified from hard and rigid to soft and pliable.

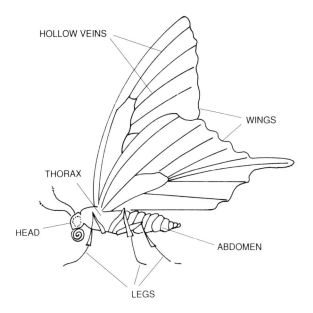

Fig. 2. Adult butterfly, stylized side view

The body of the butterfly is divided into three regions: head, thorax, and abdomen (fig. 2). The head bears a pair of antennae, two compound eyes, the labial palpi, and the proboscis, or tongue (fig. 3). The antennae are segmented and enlarged at their tips. A major function of the antennae is the detection of odors.

The compound eyes of butterflies are composed of many individual units and are particularly sensitive to the detection of movement. Most butterflies distinguish the same colors of the visible spectrum as humans do, although a few are blind to red. In addition, butterflies have vision in the ultraviolet end of the spectrum and in polarized light. Since many

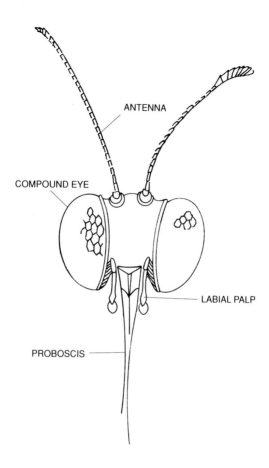

ANTENNA

COMPOUND EYE

LABIAL PALP

PROBOSCIS

Fig. 3. Butterfly head, stylized front view

flowers and butterflies reflect ultraviolet rays, a
butterfly's view of a flower or other butterflies
may be quite different from that of humans.

A pair of palpi serve as housing for the
proboscis when it is not in use and are capable

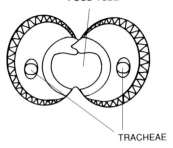

FOOD TUBE

TRACHEAE

Fig. 4. Proboscis cross section

of detecting odors. The proboscis is a long tube consisting of two parallel halves locked together like the Zip-lock closures on plastic bags (fig. 4). Muscles in the head provide a pumping action for the ingestion of nectar and other liquid foods (fig. 5). When not in use, the coiled proboscis is stored between the palpi (fig. 6).

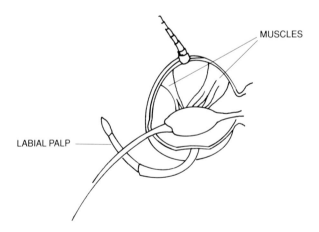

MUSCLES

LABIAL PALP

Fig. 5. Butterfly head, interior

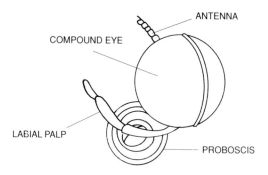

Fig. 6. Butterfly head, stylized side view

Three pairs of jointed legs and two pairs of wings are attached to the thorax. Members of the family Nymphalidae have the first pair of legs greatly reduced in size. Useless for walking or perching, the legs function as odor detectors.

The two pairs of wings are transparent membranes reinforced by hollow veins (see figure 2). The wings are covered with small partially overlapping scales, giving the appearance of a shingled roof (fig. 7). Each scale has a projection at the base which fits into a tiny cavity in the wing membranes. The major function of the scales is to stiffen the wing membranes and to provide the color pattern typical of each species.

The butterfly's abdomen is segmented, though not obviously so. Orifices for the digestive and reproductive systems are located at the tip. Males have a pair of claspers to hold the female during mating.

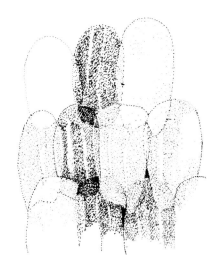

Fig. 7. Portion of butterfly wing showing overlapping scales (magnified view)

  Each side of the body of an adult butterfly or caterpillar contains a lateral row of oval openings called spiracles. These openings permit air to enter a branching set of tubes, tracheae and tracheoles, which supply oxygen to the various organs and tissues.

  The circulatory system consists of a dorsal tubular heart and small supplementary pumps located at the base of the legs and sometimes other appendages. The greenish or yellowish blood of butterflies does not contain hemoglobin. Its function is to transport hormones, nutritive materials, and excretory products, and to maintain body pressures.

Color

The bright colors and patterns of butterfly wings
are the result of the colors and arrangement of
the tiny scales covering them. Black, white,
brown, orange, yellow, and red colors are usually
due to pigments. Other scales owe their hues to
the diffraction of light from microscopic ridges
and grooves on their surface. Diffraction colors
are usually green, blue, purple, or silver. The
colors of some scales result from a combination
of pigments and diffraction.

Basic wing color and pattern helps
courting males to conserve energy by
approaching only females of the same species.
Protective coloration and pattern also reduce
the possibility of a butterfly being eaten by
predators. For example, the undersurface of
the wings of the Mourning Cloak (*Nymphalis
antiopa*) resembles dark-colored tree bark,
while those of the Hop Merchant (*Polygonia
comma*) and Question Mark (*Polygonia
interrogationis*) imitate dead leaves. Motionless,
with their wings folded, these butterflies blend
with their background and are difficult to
distinguish. During flight, only bright-colored
flashes from the upper wing surfaces are seen
by a pursuer. When the butterfly suddenly
alights with folded wings, it mysteriously
disappears from view.

Other butterflies like the Appalachian
Eyed Brown (*Satyrodes appalachia*), Common
Wood Nymph (*Cercyonis pegala*), and the Little
Wood Satyr (*Megisto cymela*) have spots along
the edges of their wings that superficially
resemble eyes. Birds tend to attack these "eyes,"
so that the resultant harm to the butterfly is

the loss of only a small amount of wing tissue. Some Hairstreaks have a false head at the base of the hind wings consisting of colored spots with tails which mimic insect heads with antennae. While the butterfly is at rest, the illusion is heightened by movement of the hind wings.

WARNING COLORATION AND MIMICRY

Some species of butterflies contain compounds that render them toxic and distasteful to birds and other predators. The Monarch (*Danaus plexippus*) is a well-known example of a butterfly that contains poisonous glycosides derived from the food plant eaten during the larval stage. Distasteful species advertise their toxic properties by means of bright colors and distinctive color patterns. For example, the bright blue and black upper wing surfaces and the prominent orange spots on the underside of the Pipe-vine Swallowtail (*Battus philenor*) warn predators of the butterfly's unpalatability. The Pipe-vine Swallowtail is the model for four Delmarva mimics: the Red-spotted Purple (*Basilarchia arthemis astyanax*), the dark female form of the Tiger Swallowtail (*Pterourus glaucus*), the female Black Swallowtail (*Papilio polyxenes asterius*), and the Spicebush Swallowtail (*Pterourus troilus*).

Some edible species have developed color patterns very close to those of the toxic model species, thus lessening the chances of being consumed by a predator. This characteristic is termed Batesian mimicry after British naturalist Henry Bates who first described it.

Two or more unpalatable species sharing the same warning color pattern represent a phenomenon known as Mullerian mimicry, first described by Fritz Muller, a German naturalist. A predator only has to learn one warning color pattern for a group of Mullerian mimics. The benefit (reduced mortality from inexperienced predators otherwise trying every species) is shared by each species.

For many years the relationship between the distasteful Monarch (*Danaus plexippus*) and the Viceroy (*Basilarchia archippus*) was thought to be one of classic Batesian mimicry. In 1991 Brower and Ritland of the University of Florida published the results of their study of Monarch-Viceroy mimicry which, surprisingly, demonstrated that both species are objectionable to birds. The relationship is, therefore, one of Mullerian rather than Batesian mimicry.

Life Cycle

The development of members of the order Lepidoptera and several other orders of insects takes place in four distinct, dissimilar stages: egg, larva, pupa, and adult. This order of development is termed complete metamorphosis. The term incomplete metamorphosis is applied to insects that have no distinct larval or pupal stages: for example, grasshoppers and crickets.

EGG

The eggs of all butterflies share a common feature: a shell with one or more tiny openings in the top called micropyles. These openings provide a means for the sperm to enter and fertilize the egg. Egg shapes are variable, ranging from smooth-surfaced spheres in the swallowtails to symmetrical but nonspherical shapes with many striations and indentations, as in the Monarch. Most eggs are white, but some are green or orange. The female usually deposits eggs on the food plant either singly or in clusters, depending upon the species.

LARVA

The larvae of butterflies and moths are called caterpillars. Basically, they are eating machines designed for rapid growth through their ability to rapidly ingest and utilize large amounts of food. The body is long and segmented (see figure 8). The head bears mouthparts consisting of a pair of strong toothed jaws and an upper and lower lip with an adjacent spinneret, a silk-producing organ. The single spinneret is centrally located on the front of the head of the caterpillar below the mandibles or jaws.

Also located on the head are a pair of very short antennae and several pairs of small, simple (not compound) eyes, termed ommatidia.

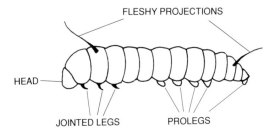

Fig. 8. Caterpillar, stylized side view

Behind the head, each of the first three body segments (corresponding to the thorax of the adult) bears a pair of jointed legs (see figure 8). Five of the following abdominal segments are furnished with pairs of fleshy prolegs. The body is often covered with spines, tubercles, fleshy projections, and hairs.

Caterpillars grow prodigiously. In order to accommodate the increase in body size, the integument, or outer skin, is shed periodically. The period between molts is termed an instar. Usually four, five, or six instars occur, but a few species have more.

The colors of caterpillars frequently vary with the instar. For example, early instars of the Spicebush Swallowtail (*Pterourus troilus*) resemble bird droppings, while the last instar is green with large false eyespots. There may also be different color phases within the same species. Because of these color variations, identification of caterpillars is sometimes very difficult. Identification may also be complicated by the possibility that the larva in question may be that of a moth or a sawfly. There are no definitive characteristics separating butterfly and moth caterpillars, but the following generalities may be helpful: caterpillars that are very hairy, those having a rhinoceroslike horn on the posterior end, or those of a very large size, usually are moth caterpillars. Larvae of foliage-consuming sawflies, a group related to bees and wasps, have only a single pair of eyes, whereas butterfly caterpillars have several pairs. Also, any caterpillarlike larva with more than six pairs of prolegs is a sawfly. Finally, positive identification can be made by rearing a larva to its adult stage.

PUPA

The term pupa (plural: pupae) refers to both butterflies and moths in the resting stage between caterpillar and adult. A butterfly pupa is also called a chrysalis. All chrysalises are pupae.

The transformation to a chrysalis marks the end of the caterpillar's last instar. At this time the caterpillar empties its digestive tract and wanders about, searching for a suitable spot to transform into a chrysalis. Most species, using the spinneret, spin a small pad of silk on a leaf, twig, plant stem, bark, or other suitable substrate and attach the last pair of prolegs to the silk pad. The caterpillar hangs head downward and assumes a J shape. Some species employ an additional support in the form of a girdle of silk. Eventually the larval skin splits, starting at the head end, and is rapidly forced backward by movements of the pupa. The tip of the abdomen has a group of tiny hooks called a cremaster which quickly becomes entangled with the threads of the silk pad. As soon as this happens, the pupal skin falls away. It may take several hours for the pupa to attain the final chrysalis shape and color.

Butterfly chrysalises vary widely in shape and color. Many are protectively colored to blend with their surroundings. Green, brown, or a mixture of gray, brown, black, yellow, and off-white are typical. Spots of silver and gold are also common. Color frequently varies within the same species.

ADULT

Even before the change from larva to pupa takes place, many adult organs and tissues have started to develop inside the caterpillar. Development accelerates during the last instar and concludes quickly in the pupal stage. When all adult organs except the wings and tongue are fully developed, air accumulates in the digestive system. Pressure increases on the pupal shell until it ruptures at the head end and the butterfly emerges. The wings are small, soft, flat pads which must be expanded to full size by pumping blood into the veins. In order for this to happen, the butterfly must position itself so that the expanding wings hang downward. Wing expansion usually does not proceed uniformly, and some areas of the wing expand more rapidly than others. This may lead to a temporarily crinkled appearance.

At first, the fully expanded wings are very soft and pliable. Hence, the butterfly remains quiescent until they have hardened, a process that takes about an hour. During this period, the two halves of the tongue are locked together, and accumulated waste products are ejected in the form of a liquid called the meconium.

Once the wings have hardened, the adult butterfly searches for suitable floral food sources, feeding on the nectar of choice or on an acceptable nonfloral food. These flights continue until it is time to fertilize and deposit the eggs, and the cycle is renewed once again.

LIFE SPAN

According to Opler and Krizek (1984), the maximum life span of temperate zone adult butterflies not overwintering as adults, that is, the length of the period between emergence from the chrysalis and death from old age, ranges from about three days (female Cabbage Butterfly *Pieris rapae*) to twenty-five days (male Alfalfa Butterfly, *Colias eurytheme*). The Monarch (*Danaus plexippus*) and other species, such as the Mourning Cloak (*Nymphalis antiopa*), Question Mark (*Polygonia interrogationis*), and Hop Merchant (*Polygonia comma*), which overwinter in the adult stage, have maximum life spans of five to eleven months. Dr. Thomas C. Emmel of the University of Florida has found that some tropical heliconiine and ithomiine butterflies can live six and eleven months respectively.

However, because of deaths from adverse weather conditions or predation by birds, spiders, and other insects, the *average* life expectancy for a butterfly species is about one-half its maximum life span.

Enemies

Butterfly populations are kept in check by a host of parasites and predators. Eggs are parasitized by tiny wasps with larvae that develop within the egg. Parasitic wasps of several families of Hymenoptera deposit their eggs inside butterfly caterpillars. Once hatched, these larvae feed on the caterpillar's body fluids and internal organs until the host dies. The larvae of some species of flies also parasitize caterpillars. The adult female fly glues its eggs to the outside of the caterpillar, and the newly hatched fly larvae burrow inside and begin feeding. Pupae also are parasitized. Caterpillars are frequently infected by a variety of viruses, bacteria, protozoa, and fungi.

Various predators—birds, lizards, toads, and many other insects—consume large numbers of adult butterflies. Arthropod predators are the most numerous, and include praying mantises, wasps, ambush bugs, assassin bugs, lacewings, robber flies, ants, tiger beetles, dragonflies, web-building spiders, and flower spiders.

It is estimated that due to the combined effects of weather, parasites, and predators, an average of only 2 percent of all butterfly eggs will become adult butterflies. Since the reproductive potential of most butterfly species is high, an average survival rate of 2 percent is usually adequate to maintain breeding populations while damaging outbreaks of defoliating caterpillars are usually avoided.

However, the most devastating enemy of butterflies is man. Through the continuing destruction of habitat in favor of housing developments, shopping malls, highways, and factories, and by the cutting of forests and draining of wetlands, butterfly populations are being inexorably diminished. Major land-disturbing activities inevitably destroy native plants and seriously disrupt or obliterate butterfly habitats, thereby reducing populations of larval and adult food sources.

In North America many butterfly species are currently threatened or endangered.

Large-scale application of pesticides also kills many butterflies. Spraying for gypsy moth, for example, can be particularly damaging to species that occur in small scattered colonies in specialized habitats within the targeted areas.

Habitats

As with other wild creatures, butterflies require suitable living space that provides not only food for caterpillars and adults but also areas for sunning, perching, courtship, and mating. Habitat size varies from many acres to a few square feet, depending largely on the abundance and distribution of the caterpillar food plants.

Suitable habitats for butterflies include relatively undisturbed bogs, marshes, woodlands, and seashores, as well as areas subject to human activity such as pastures, roadsides, railroad rights-of-way, and old fields. Butterfly habitats are not permanent in general, although if left undisturbed, they may persist for many years. Some areas, such as unused fields (originally a suitable habitat), slowly change through the normal succession of plant species and eventually become woodlands. Many suitable habitats are destroyed by farming practices and changes in land use. Habitat destruction is most serious for butterfly species that live in small, widely scattered areas and that have only a limited number of caterpillar food plants.

Climate rather than lack of habitat prevents many southern species from becoming permanent Delmarva residents. A few species such as the Buckeye (*Junonia coenia*), the Variegated Fritillary (*Euptoieta claudia*), and the Painted Lady (*Vanessa cardui*), annually arrive in late spring from their southern breeding grounds and produce one or more generations that are usually eliminated by the first severe frost. The Delmarva Peninsula provides a diversity of habitats for both resident and emigrant butterfly species. For habitat information not covered by the following discussion, please refer to the habitat section in each species account.

BEACHES AND DUNE AREAS

Butterfly populations are at their height in late summer and early fall when seaside goldenrod, purple gerardia, mistflower, and groundsel tree are in blossom. Migrating Monarchs (*Danaus plexippus*) as well as the Buckeye (*Junonia coenia*) and other Nymphalidae are usually abundant then.

Starting in early spring, congregations consisting of male individuals of the Zebra Swallowtail (*Eurytides marcellus*), Tiger Swallowtail (*Pterourus glaucus*), Spicebush Swallowtail (*Pterourus troilus*), and occasionally the Red-spotted Purple (*Basilarchia arthemis astyanax*) may be seen on undisturbed beaches, especially those of the Chesapeake Bay. It has been suggested that they may be sucking in sodium ions with the moisture.

OPEN WOODS, WOOD EDGES, AND WOODED PATHS

Delmarva's earliest spring butterflies are overwintered adults of the Mourning Cloak

(*Nymphalis antiopa*), Hop Merchant (*Polygonia comma*), and Question Mark (*Polygonia interrogationis*) species which emerge from hibernation on warm, sunny days. These are closely followed by the appearance of adults of several species that passed the winter in the pupal stage. These include the Spring Azure (*Celastrina argiolus*), Falcate Orange Tip (*Paramidea midea*), Tiger Swallowtail (*Pterourus glaucus*), Spicebush Swallowtail (*Pterourus troilus*), Zebra Swallowtail (*Eurytides marcellus*), and Brown, Frosted, Henry's, and Eastern Pine Elfin (*Incisalia augustinus, I. irus, I. henrici, and I. niphon*).

Individuals of the Red-spotted Purple (*Basilarchia arthemis astyanax*), Little Wood Satyr (*Megisto cymela*), and Common Wood Nymph (*Cercyonis pegala*) appear in late May and June.

THICK DEEP WOODS

Deep woods with little sunlight usually have very sparse butterfly populations.

WHITE CEDAR SWAMPS

The Atlantic white cedar is the sole caterpillar food plant of Hessel's Hairstreak (*Mitoura hesseli*). This species is easily overlooked because of its habit of perching high up in tall white cedars.

DISTURBED AREAS

Disturbed areas (roadsides, railroad rights-of-way, abandoned fields and pastures, power lines) are commonly rich in herbaceous plants, including many alien species. A large number of butterfly species are attracted to this type of habitat, the species varying with location and season.

MEADOWS

Wet meadows are areas that are wet most or all of the year, but do not have standing water. The vegetation in these meadows consists mainly of sedges and herbaceous plants with occasional clumps of small willows, alders, and other woody plants. The Baltimore Checkerspot (*Euphydryas phaeton*) and the Bronze Copper (*Hyllolycaena hyllus*) are typical wet meadow inhabitants.

Various grasses predominate in dry meadows along with many flowering plants attractive to butterflies. These include various species of thistle; milkweeds; several species of the genus *Eupatorium,* including mistflower, Joe-Pye-weed, and boneset; goldenrods, ironweed; and many others.

Many species of butterflies obtain nectar from this floral banquet. Usually present, although not necessarily at the same time, are all of our species of Swallowtails, Meadow Fritillary (*Clossiana bellona*), Great Spangled Fritillary (*Speyeria cybele*), Pearl Crescent (*Phyciodes tharos*), American Painted Lady (*Vanessa virginiensis*), Painted Lady (*Vanessa cardui*), Cabbage Butterfly (*Pieris rapae*), Clouded Sulphur (*Colias philodice*), and Alfalfa Butterfly (*Colias eurytheme*).

OLD FIELDS

Old fields are neglected meadows or reverting agricultural fields that have been invaded by trees and shrubs. The result is a mixture of open sunny areas ideal for herbaceous flowering plants and shaded areas, both attractive to butterflies for perching and sunning. The understory also attracts woodland butterflies such as the Little Wood Satyr (*Megisto cymela*) and the Common Wood Nymph (*Cercyonis pegala*).

Migration

Many of the butterfly species inhabiting Delmarva during spring, summer, and fall months (Buckeye [*Junonia coenia*], Variegated Fritillary [*Euptoieta claudia*], Painted Lady [*Vanessa cardui*], Red Admiral [*Vanessa atalanta rubria*], Sleepy Orange [*Eurema nicippe*], and Little Sulphur [*Eurema lisa*]) are not year-round residents. Instead, they annually migrate from the south, arriving on the Delmarva Peninsula as early as mid-April. Here they locate suitable larval food plants and start colonies that may persist until the first heavy frost. At this time, all immature stages and most adults die.

A few adults survive through a reverse migration to the south. Adults of the Red Admiral (*Vanessa atalanta rubria*) and Painted Lady (*Vanessa cardui*) are less susceptible to cold and may survive mild winters. The Cloudless Sulphur (*Phoebis sennae eubule*) migrates to this area but does not arrive until late September or October. It does not establish colonies and eventually freezes to death.

In the fall adult Monarchs (*Danaus plexippus*) leave their breeding places and migrate to warmer areas where they spend the winter. Like migrating birds, they cover long distances that require stops for rest and "refueling." Cape May State Park at Cape May, New Jersey, is a major assembly and rest stop where Monarchs have ample nectar supplies in seaside goldenrod and groundsel trees. Some winter along parts of the South Carolina and Florida coasts, while the vast majority fly on to overwintering areas in the mountains of Mexico.

In the spring survivors mate and migrate to the southern United States. There eggs are laid, and a new generation of adults is produced. This next generation continues the northward return migration and repopulates the breeding areas.

The long two-way Monarch migration is an amazing natural phenomenon. It appears even more amazing when one considers that the necessary behavior responses for migration are inherited, not learned. None of the migrants had the benefit of the knowledge and experience of previous migrants.

Some adults of the Question Mark (*Polygonia interrogationis*) and the Hop Merchant (*Polygonia comma*)—the latter to a lesser extent—migrate to the Carolinas for the winter and return in the spring. Others hibernate in Delmarva under loose bark and shingles, or in hollow logs and tree cavities.

II. SPECIES ACCOUNTS

Swallowtails
Family Papilionidae
Subfamily Papilioninae

The only members of the family Papilionidae occurring in the eastern United States are the Swallowtails, which are characterized by their large size and tails on their hind wings. Their fore wing length ranges from 2.9 to 7.6 centimeters. Eggs are smooth and nearly spherical. When threatened, the caterpillar can evert from behind the head an orange-colored, forked, defensive organ with an unpleasant scent.

The chrysalis of the Swallowtail is attached to bark, twigs, or other substrates. It may be green or a mixture of brown and gray, and unlike many other butterflies, the Swallowtail chrysalis is positioned with the head up rather than down. This is made possible by the use of a girdle of silk in addition to the usual caudal attachment. All Delmarva species overwinter in the chrysalis stage.

PIPE-VINE SWALLOWTAIL (*Battus philenor*)

Butterfly (Plates 1 and 2): The Pipe-vine
Swallowtail is Delmarva's only species having
the upper surface of the forewings mostly black,
and the upper surface of the hind wings bright,
shiny, metallic dark blue or blue green.

The adult of the Pipe-vine Swallowtail is
distasteful to predators and is mimicked by six
palatable species. Four of these occur in Delmarva:
the Red-spotted Purple (*Basilarchia arthemis
astyanax*), the female Spicebush Swallowtail
(*Pterourus troilus*), the dark female form of the
Tiger Swallowtail (*Pterourus glaucus*), and the
female Black Swallowtail (*Papilio polyxenes
asterius*). Of these the Red-spotted Purple is the
closest mimic, but it can be readily distinguished
by its lack of tails and, in common with the
other mimics, a blue color that is not iridescent.

Range: This species occurs from near the tip of
Florida to central New England and westward
to the Mississippi River; beyond the Mississippi
the northern edge of the range slants southward
across Missouri into Mexico and extends to the
Pacific Ocean.

Habitat: On the Delmarva Peninsula, this
Swallowtail is usually found along roadsides, in
open fields, and in gardens where flowers are
abundant. It is uncommon on the peninsula,
probably because of the scarcity of the larval
food plant.

Adult Food Sources: Thistles, milkweeds, and
butterfly bush are favorites. Lilacs, phlox,

dame's rocket, petunia, bergamot and other nectar sources are also visited.

Immature Stages (Plates 95 and 96): Reddish brown eggs are deposited in clusters on the food plant. Only two larval food plants are available in Delmarva. These are dutchman's pipe and Virginia snakeroot. Dutchman's pipe is not native to Delmarva but is occasionally cultivated as an ornamental. Virginia snakeroot is native but occurs only infrequently. Contrary to some references, wild ginger is not utilized as a larval food plant.

Young caterpillars feed together in groups but separate when they get older. All instars are similar in appearance. The basic color is dark, reddish brown with fleshy tubercles of the same color arranged in two rows. The chrysalis is marked by yellow or purplish patches on a greenish or brownish background. There are three broods annually.

ZEBRA SWALLOWTAIL *(Eurytides marcellus)*

Butterfly (Plate 3): The black-and-white Zebra Swallowtail is Delmarva's only representative of a group of tropical Swallowtails characterized by hind wings with very long narrow tails. No other species found here resemble it. The first individuals to emerge in early spring from over-wintering pupae are smaller than the summer individuals and have much shorter tails; otherwise, they are similar.

Range: The range of the Zebra Swallowtail extends westward from northern New Jersey

and northwestern New York along the southern
edges of the Great Lakes to Minnesota and
south to Florida and the Gulf of Mexico.

Habitat: The Zebra Swallowtail is found in
woodlands that contain the pawpaw, its only
larval food. It is also found in nearby fields and
gardens where it searches for nectar sources.

Adult Food Sources: In early spring this
butterfly feeds on dandelions, blueberries, lilacs,
and redbud. Later generations visit milkweeds,
dogbanes, red clover, and other flowering plants.

Immature Stages (Plates 97 and 98): The
spherical eggs are deposited on leaves of the
pawpaw. Mature caterpillars have two color
phases. One phase has a light green body with
one narrow band of yellow and another of black
near the anterior end, followed by a series of
very fine yellow bands. The other phase has a
black body with narrow bands of yellow and pale
blue along the entire length. The chrysalis may
be either pale green or brown. Two generations
occur per year.

BLACK SWALLOWTAIL (*Papilio polyxenes
asterius*)

Butterfly (Plates 4, 5, and 6): The male Black
Swallowtail is easily identified by the yellow
band on the upper side of both wings. This is
absent or reduced to a row of dots on the female.
The blue area on the upper hind wings is small
in the male but large and quite prominent in the
female. At close range both can be positively

identified by the occurrence of a small round orange dot with a black dot in its center on the lower edge of the hind wings on the upper surface.

Range: This Swallowtail ranges throughout the United States east of the Mississippi River.

Habitat: The Black Swallowtail frequents many habitats including open fields, fence rows, pastures, roadsides, and gardens.

Adult Food Sources: This species visits a wide variety of plants to obtain nectar. Its favorites include milkweeds, New York ironweed, thistles, butterfly bush, and zinnia.

Immature Stages (Plates 99, 100, and 101): The female deposits spherical eggs on the food plant. Newly hatched caterpillars are predominantly black. Some green appears in later stages. Fully grown caterpillars are bright green with a series of black rings and yellow or orange dots. The chrysalis is either green with yellow markings, or mottled brown or gray.

Wild or cultivated carrots are the favorite food plants, but other members of the parsley family, including dill, parsley, celery, and parsnip, also are utilized. Damage to cultivated crops is seldom serious. There are three generations per year.

TIGER SWALLOWTAIL *(Pterourus glaucus)*

Butterfly (Plates 8, 9, 10, and 11): Males of this colorful and common Swallowtail are easily identified by their "tiger" pattern of yellow and black stripes. Females closely resemble the males except for a large area of blue on the hind wings above. This is very small or absent in males. A mimetic, dark, female form of the Tiger Swallowtail occurs in areas where the Pipe-vine Swallowtail (*Battus philenor*) is also found. (See discussion in Pipe-vine Swallowtail species account.)

In flight the dark form is difficult to distinguish from females of the Spicebush Swallowtail (*Pterourus troilus*) or the Black Swallowtail (*Papilio polyxenes asterius*). It differs from them in its larger size and greater expanse of blue above. Close examination of the underside will reveal that the striped pattern of the yellow form is preserved but in black and dark brown. The Tiger Swallowtail, like the Zebra Swallowtail (*Eurytides marcellus*), has an early spring population with smaller adults than later generations.

Range: The Tiger Swallowtail inhabits all of the United States east of the Continental Divide and eastern Canada south of Hudson Bay. West of the Great Lakes, the Canadian population extends northwest as far as central Alaska.

Habitat: The Tiger Swallowtail usually will be found in deciduous woods, along woods' edges and sunny paths, or in nearby open fields. However, it is a strong, vigorous flier and frequently visits gardens in towns and cities.

Adult Food Sources: Favorite nectar sources include milkweeds, thistles, ironweeds,

Joe-Pye-weed, buttonbush, sweet pepperbush, Turk's-cap lily, Japanese honeysuckle, lilacs, and butterfly bush.

Immature Stages (Plates 102 and 103): The female deposits spherical eggs on leaves of the host plant. Small caterpillars are mostly black; fully grown caterpillars are a medium shade of green with two distinct "eyespots." They spend daytime hours in a shelter formed by rolling a leaf into a tube and securing it with silk. They leave the shelter at night to feed.

The chrysalis may be green or a mixture of brown and gray. Leaves of a wide variety of woody plants also serve as food. Tulip poplar is a favorite in Delmarva. Others are sweet bay, wild cherry, spicebush, sassafras, and ash. There are two broods per year.

SPICEBUSH SWALLOWTAIL (*Pterourus troilus*)

Butterfly (Plates 12, 13, and 14): Males of the Spicebush Swallowtail are easily identified in flight by the large area of bluish green (occasionally blue) on the upper side of the hind wings. In females some of the green is replaced by blue. Close inspection may be required to distinguish the latter from females of the Black Swallowtail (*Papilio polyxenes asterius*) and the dark form of the Tiger Swallowtail (*Pterourus glaucus*). The female Spicebush Swallowtail has a prominent orange dot on the front edge of the hind wing above. This dot is not present in the female Black Swallowtail. The dark form of the Tiger Swallowtail is larger and has a more extensive blue area on the upper hind wings; furthermore, the crescent-shaped spots along the edge of the hind wing are green in the Spicebush Swallowtail and yellow in the others.

Range: The Spicebush Swallowtail occurs from central New England west to the Mississippi and south to the tip of the Florida peninsula.

Habitat: This common species is found in woodlands and in fields and gardens bordering or near woods.

Adult Food Sources: A wide variety of flowers are visited. Some favorites are milkweeds, dogbane, sweet pepperbush, thistles, ironweeds, and Japanese honeysuckle. Dandelions are visited in early spring.

Immature Stages (Plates 104 and 105): Eggs are deposited on the food plant. The early instars are black with some white and bear a remarkable resemblance to bird droppings. Succeeding instars are lighter with increasing amounts of green. When fully grown, the caterpillar is green with two eyespots and six rows of blue dots. Just before pupation the green areas become bright orange or yellow. The caterpillar feeds mostly at night, spending daylight hours in a tubular shelter made from a leaf. The chrysalis may be either green or brown.
Sassafras and spicebush are the usual foods of caterpillars of this species on the Delmarva Peninsula.

PALAMEDES SWALLOWTAIL (*Pterourus palamedes*)

Butterfly (Plate 15): The upper surface of the wings of the Palamedes Swallowtail is black with a broad yellow stripe crossing both wings and a row of yellow dots along the wing edges. It differs from the male Black Swallowtail (*Papilio polyxenes asterius*) in its larger size, the absence of the orange dot with black center (present on the upper hind wing of the Black Swallowtail), and the presence of yellow stripes instead of dots on the body.

Range: The range of the Palamedes Swallowtail extends southward along the coastal plain from southern Delmarva to eastern Texas.

Habitat: This Swallowtail favors swampy woods and other wet areas where its larval food plants, red bay and sweet bay, are common.

Adult Food Sources: Favorite nectar sources are sweet pepperbush, azaleas, various thistles, and blue flag.

Immature Stages: Eggs are deposited on red bay, the preferred larval food plant. The fully grown caterpillar is green with small blue spots resembling the larva of the Spicebush Swallowtail (*Pterourus troilus*). Also, like the Spicebush Swallowtail larvae, Palamedes larvae construct shelters from partially rolled leaves covered with a mat of silk. There are two generations per year.

Whites, Orange Tips, and Sulphurs
Family Pieridae

Members of this family are either white with black markings like the Cabbage Butterfly (*Pieris rapae*) or various shades of yellow and orange with black markings like the Clouded Sulphur (*Colias philodice*) and the Alfalfa Butterfly (*Colias eurytheme*). The Falcate Orange Tip (*Paramidia midea*) is an exception having white wings with orange tips in the male. The length of the forewing ranges from 1.5 to 3.5 centimeters. Eggs are usually longer than broad, are frequently ribbed, and resemble a smaller copy of the Monarch's (*Danaus plexippus*) eggs. Whites, including the Orange Tip, generally feed on plants of the mustard family in their larval stage while Sulphurs prefer legumes. Caterpillars are usually slender, hairless, and green with long stripes. The chrysalis is anchored by a silk girdle plus the usual silk button. The winter is passed in the chrysalis stage.

Whites: Subfamily Pierinae

CHECKERED WHITE (*Pontia protodice*)

Butterfly (Plates 16 and 17): White is the predominant color of both sexes. The upper surface of the male forewing has several black spots, the largest being roughly rectangular in shape. The hind wing has no spots. The female is quite different, having a "checkered" pattern of black on both wings above. The similar looking Cabbage Butterfly (*Pieris rapae*) has a black wing tip and one (male) or two (female) black dots on the upper wing surface.

Range: The Checkered White can be found over most of the United States east of the Mississippi with the exception of northern New England and northern New York State.

Habitat: Dry, open areas such as abandoned and uncultivated fields, railroad tracks, and open sandy areas near beaches are preferred. In the Delmarva region, the Checkered White is sometimes locally common, but these colonies do not persist.

Adult Food Sources: Milkweeds and various species of mustards and cresses are preferred.

Immature Stages: Yellow eggs are laid on the food plant. The caterpillar is blue green with yellow stripes and feeds on a number of plants of the mustard family. These include shepherd's purse, peppergrass, and watercress. The chrysalis is blue gray with black specks. The Checkered White has three and sometimes a partial fourth generation, which produces fewer adults than the earlier three.

CABBAGE BUTTERFLY (*Pieris rapae*)

Butterfly (Plate 18): Accidentally introduced from Europe, the Cabbage Butterfly is now by far Delmarva's most common predominantly white species. Distinguishing marks are the black wing tips and the black spots on the upper side of the forewing, one in the male, two in the female.

Range: This butterfly can be found throughout the United States.

Habitat: The Cabbage Butterfly frequents flower and vegetable gardens and open fields, particularly where the caterpillar food plants occur.

Adult Food Sources: The butterfly visits an extremely wide variety of floral nectar sources. These include dandelion, various mustards, butterfly bush, red clover, and aster, as well as bergamot and the members of the mint family.

Immature Stages: As its name suggests, caterpillars of the Cabbage Butterfly thrive on cabbage, but other members of the mustard family are also utilized as food. These include broccoli, cauliflower, Brussels sprouts, watercress, peppergrass, and various wild mustards. Nasturtiums are sometimes consumed also.

The green eggs are deposited on the food plant. Caterpillars are green with a narrow yellow line down the middle of the back and another on each side. The chrysalis also is green. This butterfly reproduces constantly from early spring to November.

Orange Tips: Subfamily Anthocharinae

FALCATE ORANGE TIP (*Paramidia midea*)

Butterfly (Plates 19 and 20): The common name of this attractive small butterfly is derived from the sickle (falcate) shape of the tip of the

forewing plus an orange wing tip in the male.
The adult butterfly emerges from the chrysalis
during the last two weeks of April and the first
two weeks of May. Males live a maximum of two
weeks while females survive for only three to
four days. There is a single brood annually.

Range: The Falcate Orange Tip ranges from
western Massachusetts and Connecticut south
along the coast to Florida and west to central
Texas and also to parts of Wisconsin and Missouri.

Habitat: In Delmarva, the Falcate Orange Tip
frequents open woodlands and the edges of
roads bordering or passing through woods. It is
not uniformly distributed but occurs in scattered
local colonies.

Adult Food Sources: The Falcate Orange Tip
prefers small white flowers such as field
chickweed, winter and other cresses, peppergrass,
and wild strawberry. Dandelions, cut-leaved
toothwort, and violets also are visited.

Immature Stages: The orange colored eggs of
the Falcate Orange Tip are deposited singly on
the food plant. With age, the color of caterpillars
progresses from yellow green to blue green. An
orange stripe runs down the middle of the back,
and there are white stripes on the sides.
    The chrysalis is green, narrow, and sharply
pointed at both ends. The caterpillars' food is
limited to plants of the mustard family— mainly
various cresses and mustards and cut-leaved
toothwort. There is one generation annually.

Sulphurs: Subfamily Coliadinae

CLOUDED SULPHUR (*Colias philodice*)
ALFALFA BUTTERFLY (*Colias eurytheme*)

Butterfly (Plates 21, 22, and 23): These two
species are described together because of their
many strong similarities. In fact, they are so
similar that hybridization occasionally occurs.
The most obvious difference between adults of
the two species is the color of the wings above:
yellow in the Clouded Sulphur and orange or
mixed orange and yellow in the Alfalfa Butterfly,
also known as the Orange Sulphur. In both
species the wings have a distinct black border:
solid black in males but dotted with yellow in
females. Each species has a female white form
which cannot be reliably separated by physical
appearance.

Range: The Alfalfa Butterfly occurs throughout
the continental United States with the exception
of Alaska. The Clouded Sulphur's range is
similar except that it extends into Alaska and is
not found in southern Florida.

Habitat: Both species frequent open areas,
particularly clover and alfalfa fields, as well as
meadows and roadsides.

Adult Food Sources: Nectar sources are the
same for both species. Flowers commonly visited
are dandelions, alfalfa, clovers, thistles,
milkweeds, fall asters, and some goldenrods.

Immature Stages: Eggs of both species are white and are deposited on the food plant. Caterpillars are green with a dark stripe down the back and light stripes on the sides. There is some difference in food plant preference; the larvae of the Clouded Sulphur prefer white clover, while those of the Alfalfa Butterfly feed on alfalfa, white clover, white sweet clover, and various vetches. The chrysalises are green. The Clouded Sulphur has three to five generations; the Alfalfa Butterfly has four to five.

CLOUDLESS SULPHUR (*Phoebis sennae eubule*)

Butterfly (Plate 24): The Cloudless Sulphur is the largest yellow butterfly found on the Delmarva Peninsula. Its upper side is entirely yellow. Underneath it is yellow with some reddish brown markings and two small circular spots on the hind wings.

Range: The Cloudless Sulphur is a breeding resident in Florida, southern South Carolina, Georgia, the Gulf States, and west to California. In the fall it frequently migrates northward, reaching Delmarva in late August and September; however, it cannot survive the winter here and does not reproduce here.

Habitat: The Cloudless Sulphur favors large sunny areas including gardens, beaches, roadsides, and open fields.

Adult Food Sources: Long tubular flowers are preferred by the Cloudless Sulphur, which has been reported to visit lantana, wild morning glories, and cardinal flowers.

Immature Stages (Plates 106 and 107): The Cloudless Sulphur frequently immigrates to Delmarva in late fall from farther south, but does not reproduce here. The female deposits eggs singly on the food plants of various species of sennas. Larvae may be either yellow or green with a yellow lateral stripe and black dots in crosswise rows on each side. The chrysalis is green or pink. The middle section has a large bulge that gives it a "pregnant" appearance.

LITTLE SULPHUR (*Eurema lisa*)

Butterfly (Plate 25): The Little Sulphur is Delmarva's only small, predominantly yellow butterfly. Its wing spread is about three-fourths that of the Clouded Sulphur. Upper wing surfaces are clear yellow with a heavy marginal black band.

Range: Resident populations extend from the southeastern corner of Virginia through the Carolinas, Georgia, Florida, the Gulf States, and eastern Texas. The Little Sulphur is another southern species that commonly immigrates northward in the summer and establishes temporary colonies.

Habitat: The Little Sulphur frequents dry areas, including abandoned fields, roadsides, railroad rights-of-way, and sunny woodland paths.

Adult Food Sources: In common with most small butterflies, the Little Sulphur prefers initially to seek out small flowers where the nectar is easily reached.

Immature Stages: The light green eggs are deposited singly on the food plant. Fully grown caterpillars are green with one or two white lines on each side. They feed on sennas, partridge pea, and sensitive plant. The pupa is green with black dots.

SLEEPY ORANGE (*Eurema nicippe*)

Butterfly (Plate 26): With wings bright orange bordered with black, the Sleepy Orange resembles the male Alfalfa Butterfly (*Colias eurytheme*). It may be distinguished from that species by the irregular edge of the dorsal black band and the absence of the circular dot on the hind wing below.

Range: The resident breeding areas of the Sleepy Orange are the eastern halves of North Carolina, South Carolina, and southern Georgia; Florida and the Gulf States; and west through southern Texas into California. In late summer the butterfly sometimes emigrates and may establish temporary colonies as far north as Massachusetts.

Habitat: The Sleepy Orange frequents woods' edges, old fields, and wet meadows.

Adult Food Sources: A wide variety of flowers are visited. Males frequently congregate at the edges of puddles.

Immature Stages (Plates 108 and 109): Pale green eggs are laid singly on leaves or flower buds of the host plant. Various species of senna are used as food. Larvae are slender, green, and downy.

Gossamer Wings
Family Lycaenidae

The Delmarva members of this family are divided into four subfamilies: Harvesters (subfamily Miletinae), Coppers (subfamily Lycaeninae), Hairstreaks and Elfins (subfamily Theclinae), and Blues (subfamily Polyommatinae). The forewing measures from 0.97 to 2.4 centimeters.

The Harvesters are a unique group in which the larvae are carnivorous, feeding exclusively on aphids. There is only one species in the United States.

Many Coppers—particularly the males— have upper wing surfaces that are bright orange red or purplish. The caterpillars of both species found in Delmarva feed on plants of the genus *Rumex* (sheep sorrel, curled dock, and water dock).

For purposes of description and identification, the Hairstreak group may be further divided into those that have "Hairstreak" as part of their common name and those that are called "Elfins." The upper wing surfaces of members of the Hairstreak group are mostly dark brown or gray. In a few species there are areas of blue. The undersurface may be brown, gray, black, or green depending upon the species, with black or brown dots or stripes. There is usually an orange or blue spot near the base of the hairlike tails. With the exception of the Gray Hairstreak *(Strymon melinus)*, the wings are closed when not in flight. Caterpillars frequently consume the buds or flowers of the host plant rather than the foliage. Some species are attended by ants attracted by a sugary secretion. Pupae are short and stout, usually mottled brown in color. Depending upon the species, they overwinter in the egg or chrysalis stage.

All Elfins have a single generation each year that emerges in early spring. Upper wing surfaces are gray or brown, sometimes with patches of light brown. The wings are mottled in various shades of brown and gray on the undersides. Elfin species found on Delmarva are not brightly colored and do not have hairlike tails like the Hairstreaks. Pupae are small, short, and rotund as in the Hairstreaks.

As the name "Blue" implies, this group of the Family Lycaenidae usually have blue or partially blue upper wing surfaces. An exception is the summer female of the Eastern Tailed Blue *(Everes comyntas)* which is slate gray above.

Caterpillars feed on tree buds, flowers, and immature seeds of tree host plants. Some species secrete a sugary liquid consumed by ants. In return, the ants are believed to protect the caterpillars from parasites.

Harvesters: Subfamily Miletinae

HARVESTER (*Feniseca tarquinius*)

Butterfly (Plate 27): The appearance of the adult Harvester is unique. The upper surface is orange brown with wide black borders on the forewing and the anterior edge of the hind wing. At rest with wings folded it is easily recognized by the undersides of the hind wings which are covered with many brown dots, narrowly edged with white or light-colored border.

Range: The Harvester occurs throughout the United States east of the Mississippi River and north into southern Canada.

Habitat: The Harvester frequents deciduous woodlands, particularly those areas near streams.

Adult Food Sources: This butterfly prefers aphid honeydew but also feeds on bird droppings and animal dung. Its unusually short tongue is apparently designed for feeding on honeydew.

Immature Stages: Eggs of the Harvester are greenish white and are deposited on the undersides of leaves of the host plant of the woolly aphid. The caterpillars feed exclusively on several species of woolly aphids that feed on alder, beech, ash, and witch hazel. They have faint olive stripes on a green brown background and are sparsely covered with long white hairs. The color pattern is usually obscured by a dusting of the white wax secreted by the woolly aphids. The chrysalis is greenish brown with irregular dark patches. The Harvester has three broods yearly.

Coppers: Subfamily Lycaeninae

LITTLE COPPER (*Lycaena phlaeas*)

Butterfly (Plates 28 and 29): The Little Copper is one of the most beautiful of common small butterflies. It is thought to have been accidentally introduced from Scandinavia in colonial times. The Little Copper can easily be identified by the bright orange red background of the black spotted forewing above and the spotted gray hind wing with a red margin below.

Range: The Little Copper occurs throughout southern Canada as far west as Manitoba, south to northern sections of Georgia, and in parts of Tennessee and Arkansas. Scattered populations also occur in the western United States.

Habitat: Open fields, meadows, roadsides, pastures, and gardens are favored by the Little Copper.

Adult Food Sources: The Little Copper visits a wide variety of flowers including white clover, milkweeds, yarrow, Joe-Pye-weeds, and wild sunflowers.

Immature Stages: The light green eggs are deposited on sheep sorrel and curled dock. Caterpillars are slug shaped and green or rosy red in color. The chrysalis is light brown with black spots. There are three broods of the Little Copper annually.

BRONZE COPPER (*Hyllolycaena hyllus*)

Butterfly (Plates 30, 31, and 32): The Bronze Copper can be distinguished from the Little Copper by its larger size and white hind wing underside which has black dots and a distinct orange red marginal band. The upper sides of the forewings are purplish brown in the male and pale orange brown with black dots in the female.

Range: The Bronze Copper ranges from southern Canada to Maryland and west to Alberta, Montana, and Colorado.

Habitat: This butterfly prefers marshes and wet meadows.

Adult Food Sources: The Bronze Copper occasionally visits red clover, milkweeds, and blackberry.

Immature Stages: The eggs are light green and laid on leaves of the food plants: water dock and curled dock. The caterpillar is slug shaped, yellow green, and has a dark stripe on its back. The chrysalis is orange brown with darker blotches. There are three broods each year.

Hairstreaks and Elfins: Subfamily Theclinae

GREAT PURPLE HAIRSTREAK (*Atlides halesus*)

Butterfly (Plate 33): The "Great Blue Hairstreak" would be a more appropriate common name as the upper wing surfaces of this beautiful butterfly are a brilliant iridescent blue. Below, the wings are jet black with three bright red orange dots at the base of the wing.

Range: The range of the Great Purple Hairstreak extends from central New Jersey south through the Delmarva Peninsula, the Carolinas, Georgia, northern Florida, and the Gulf States. It also occurs in California.

Habitat: The Great Purple Hairstreak inhabits wet woodlands and their edges.

Adult Food Sources: The preferred nectar sources are goldenrod, sweet pepperbush, and Hercules' club.

Immature Stages: There is little information on the size and color of eggs. The slightly downy caterpillars are green with lighter green stripes on sides and back, and a yellowish stripe low on the sides. The number of broods in Delmarva is probably two, but this is not known with certainty. They feed exclusively on mistletoe.

CORAL HAIRSTREAK (*Harkenclenus titus*)

Butterfly (Plate 34): Most Hairstreaks have one or more tiny hairlike tails on their hind wings, but the Coral Hairstreak has none. The upper wing surface is uniformly gray brown in the male. The female has a row of orange spots on the upper side of the hind wing. A row of orange or red dots along the edge of the hind wing on the underside distinguishes this species. Females are slightly larger and have more rounded wings than males.

Range: The range of the Coral Hairstreak extends from southern Canada to Florida and westward to California and British Columbia.

Habitat: The Coral Hairstreak frequents open fields, meadows, and roadsides.

Adult Food Sources: This Hairstreak has a strong preference for orange milkweed. It also visits other milkweeds, dogbane, white sweet clover, and New Jersey tea.

Immature Stages (Plate 110): The pale green eggs of the Coral Hairstreak are deposited on twigs of the host plant. The caterpillars feed on the foliage of wild cherry and wild plum. They are slug shaped and green with red patches at both the anterior and posterior ends. They are usually attended by ants attracted by a sugary substance the caterpillars secrete. The chrysalis is light brown with numerous small black spots. The Coral Hairstreak has one generation per year.

BANDED HAIRSTREAK (*Satyrium calanus*)

Butterfly (Plate 35): This usually common species is uniformly gray brown above. The background color beneath varies from a medium gray to almost black with a line of darker oblong spots outlined with white. Near the tails are a blue spot and one or two orange spots.

Range: The Banded Hairstreak is found from southern Canada south to central Florida and in west central Texas and Colorado.

Habitat: Open woods and fields, roadsides, railroad rights-of-way, and parks are frequented by the Banded Hairstreak.

Adult Food Sources: The Banded Hairstreak obtains nectar from milkweeds, dogbane, New Jersey tea, yarrow, meadowsweet, and white sweet clover.

Immature Stages: Pale green eggs are laid on twigs of the host plant. Caterpillars of this species may be either green or brown with lighter lines. They feed on oak, black walnut, and butternut leaves. There is one brood annually.

KING'S HAIRSTREAK (*Satyrium kingi*)

Butterfly: King's Hairstreak is extremely rare in Delmarva. It resembles the Striped Hairstreak (*Satyrium liparops*) but may be distinguished from it by an irregularity in the edge of the hind wing in front of the base of the tail.

Range: King's Hairstreak inhabits the coastal areas of southern Maryland, the southeast corner of Virginia, the Carolinas and Georgia, and the Florida panhandle. It also occurs in hilly and mountainous areas of the Gulf States.

Habitat: King's Hairstreak prefers coastal plains, swamps, and deciduous woods in elevated areas.

Adult Food Sources: King's Hairstreak has been observed feeding on the flowers of sourwood.

Immature Stages: The caterpillars of King's Hairstreak are green, resembling those of the Striped Hairstreak. They feed only on sweetleaf (also called horse-sugar) and have a single brood annually.

STRIPED HAIRSTREAK (*Satyrium liparops*)

Butterfly (Plate 36): The Striped Hairstreak is easily identified by a series of broken white lines on the underside of its wings that give it a striped appearance. It also has an orange cap on the blue spot on the hind wing beneath. This cap is lacking in the Banded Hairstreak *(Satyrium calanus).*

Range: The range of the Striped Hairstreak extends from southern Canada south to central Florida and west to Texas.

Habitat: The Striped Hairstreak frequents openings and edges of deciduous woods.

Adult Food Sources: The Striped Hairstreak visits milkweeds, dogbane, New Jersey tea, white sweet clover, and goldenrods.

Immature Stages: The reddish purple eggs are deposited on host twigs and buds. They do not hatch until the following spring. Caterpillars are green with yellow green oblique stripes. Their food plants include chokeberry, shadbush, wild plum, wild cherry, apple, and blackberry.

RED-BANDED HAIRSTREAK (*Calycopis cecrops*)

Butterfly (Plate 37): The Red-banded Hairstreak is most easily recognized when at rest or sunning and the wings are closed. In this position, it is easily identified by the vivid red band on both wings. In flight the basal blue of the upper side of the hind wings will be seen.

Range: The range of the Red-banded Hairstreak is from Long Island south to the Florida Keys and west to eastern Texas.

Habitat: The Red-banded Hairstreak frequents woodland edges, fields, and other noncultivated areas with small trees and shrubs.

Adult Food Sources: The Red-banded Hairstreak visits a wide variety of flowers. These include milkweeds, sumac, New Jersey tea, sweet pepperbush, dogbane, and wild cherry.

Immature Stages: The white eggs are not deposited on the host plant but are placed under dead leaves on the ground beneath the host plant. Caterpillars are dark brown with a blue green stripe on the back. Food plants include

staghorn and dwarf sumacs, oaks, and wax
myrtle. There are two generations each year.

OLIVE HAIRSTREAK (*Mitoura grynea*)

Butterfly (Plate 38): The Olive Hairstreak is
very similar in appearance to Hessel's Hairstreak
(*Mitoura hesseli*). Both are predominantly green
underneath with some brown and white lines
and dots. The green on the underside of the
Olive Hairstreak's hind wing has a hint of
yellow. The definitive difference is in the band of
white dots across the underside of the forewing.
In the Olive Hairstreak, the top dot is aligned
with the second dot, but in Hessel's Hairstreak
it is offset upward.

Range: The range of the Olive Hairstreak
extends from the southern tip of Maine south to
mid-Florida and westward to Minnesota and
Texas.

Habitat: The Olive Hairstreak likes abandoned
fields and serpentine barrens in the proximity of
red cedar trees.

Adult Food Sources: Preferences are winter
cress, milkweeds, white sweet clover, and
dogbane.

Immature Stage: The eggs of the Olive
Hairstreak are light green. They are deposited
on leaves of the host plant. Caterpillars are dark
green with light green oblique lines on each
side. They feed only on red cedar. A distinct
spring brood is followed later by occasional
emergences until the end of summer.

PLATES

Adult forms of the various species are shown
beginning with plate 1 on the next page;
selected examples of larvae, pupae, and eggs
start with plate 95.

1. Pipe-vine
 Swallowtail
Battus philenor
Dorsal view

2. Pipe-vine
 Swallowtail
Battus philenor
Ventral view

3. Zebra Swallowtail
Eurytides marcellus
Dorsal view

4. Black Swallowtail
*Papilio polyxenes
 asterius*
Female dorsal view

5. Black Swallowtail
*Papilio polyxenes
asterius*
Male dorsal view

6. Black Swallowtail
*Papilio polyxenes
asterius*
Male ventral view

7. Giant Swallowtail
Heraclides cresphontes
Dorsal view

8. Tiger Swallowtail
Pterourus glaucus
Yellow form female
dorsal view

9. Tiger Swallowtail
Pterourus glaucus
Yellow form male
   dorsal view

10. Tiger Swallowtail
Pterourus glaucus
Dark form female
   dorsal view

11. Tiger Swallowtail
Pterourus glaucus
Dark form female
   ventral view

12. Spicebush
   Swallowtail
Pterourus troilus
Female dorsal view

13. Spicebush
    Swallowtail
    Pterourus troilus
    Female ventral view

14. Spicebush
    Swallowtail
    Pterourus troilus
    Male dorsal view

15. Palamedes
    Swallowtail
    Pterourus palamedes
    Dorsal view

16. Checkered White
    Pontia protodice
    Female ventral view

17. Checkered White
Pontia protodice
Male dorsal view

18. Cabbage Butterfly
Pieris rapae
Ventral view

19. Falcate Orange Tip
Paramidia midea
Female dorsal and
        ventral views

20. Falcate Orange Tip
Paramidia midea
Male dorsal view

21. Clouded Sulphur
Colias philodice
Ventral view

22. Alfalfa Butterfly
Colias eurytheme
Ventral view

23. Alfalfa Butterfly
Colias eurytheme
White form ventral view

24. Cloudless Sulphur
Phoebis sennae eubule
Ventral view

25. Little Sulphur
Eurema lisa
Ventral view

26. Sleepy Orange
Eurema nicippe
Ventral view

27. Harvester
Feniseca tarquinius
Ventral view

28. Little Copper
Lycaena phlaeas
Dorsal view

29. Little Copper
Lycaena phlaeas
Ventral view

30. Bronze Copper
Hyllolycaena hyllus
Female dorsal view

31. Bronze Copper
Hyllolycaena hyllus
Male dorsal view

32. Bronze Copper
Hyllolycaena hyllus
Male ventral view

33. Great Purple
    Hairstreak
Atlides halesus
Ventral view

34. Coral Hairstreak
Harkenclenus titus
Ventral view

35. Banded
    Hairstreak
Satyrium calanus
Ventral view

36. Striped
    Hairstreak
Satyrium liparops
Ventral view

37. Red-banded
    Hairstreak
Calycopis cecrops
Ventral view

38. Olive Hairstreak
Mitoura grynea
Ventral view

39. Hessel's Hairstreak
Mitoura hesseli
Ventral view

40. Brown Elfin
Incisalia augustinus
Ventral view

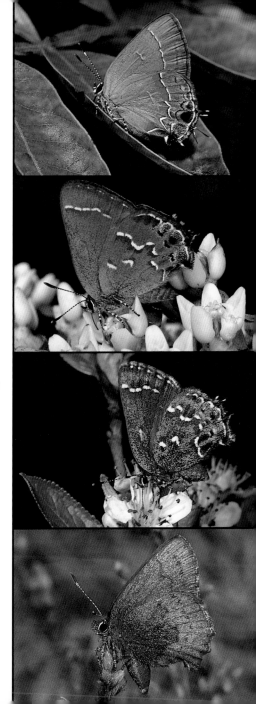

41. Frosted Elfin
Incisalia irus
Ventral view

42. Henry's Elfin
Incisalia henrici
Ventral view

43. Eastern Pine Elfin
Incisalia niphon
Ventral view

44. Northern Hairstreak
Fixsenia ontario
Ventral view

45. White-M Hairstreak
Parrhasius m-album
Ventral view

46. Gray Hairstreak
Strymon melinus
Ventral view

47. Eastern Tailed Blue
Everes comyntas
Female dorsal view

48. Eastern Tailed Blue
Everes comyntas
Spring form female
  dorsal view

49. Eastern Tailed Blue
Everes comyntas
Male dorsal view

50. Eastern Tailed Blue
Everes comyntas
Female/male ventral
    view

51. Spring Azure
Celastrina argiolus
Female dorsal view

52. Spring Azure
Celastrina argiolus
Male ventral view

53. Snout Butterfly
Libytheana bachmanii
Ventral view

54. Gulf Fritillary
Agraulis vanillae
Female dorsal view

55. Variegated
    Fritillary
Euptoieta claudia
Dorsal view

56. Great Spangled
    Fritillary
Speyeria cybele
Dorsal view

57. Great Spangled
    Fritillary
Speyeria cybele
Ventral view

58. Regal Fritillary
Speyeria idalia
Male dorsal view

59. Regal Fritillary
Speyeria idalia
Female dorsal view

60. Silver-bordered
    Fritillary
Clossiana selene
Dorsal view

61. Silver-bordered
    Fritillary
Clossiana selene
Ventral view

62. Meadow Fritillary
Clossiana bellona
Dorsal view

63. Meadow Fritillary
Clossiana bellona
Ventral view

64. Silvery Checkerspot
Charidryas nycteis
Dorsal view

65. Silvery
 Checkerspot
Charidryas nycteis
Ventral view

66. Pearl Crescent
Phyciodes tharos
Dorsal view

67. Pearl Crescent
Phyciodes tharos
Ventral view

68. Baltimore
 Checkerspot
Euphydryas phaeton
Dorsal view

69. Question Mark
*Polygonia
  interrogationis*
Summer form dorsal
  view

70. Question Mark
*Polygonia
  interrogationis*
Summer form ventral
  view

71. Question Mark
*Polygonia
  interrogationis*
Fall form dorsal view

72. Hop Merchant
Polygonia comma
Summer form dorsal
  view

73. Hop Merchant
Polygonia comma
Summer form ventral
view

74. Hop Merchant
Polygonia comma
Fall form dorsal view

75. Mourning Cloak
Nymphalis antiopa
Dorsal view

76. Milbert's Tortoise
Shell
Aglais milberti
Dorsal view

77. American Painted
    Lady
Vanessa virginiensis
Dorsal view

78. American Painted
    Lady
Vanessa virginiensis
Ventral view

79. Painted Lady
Vanessa cardui
Dorsal view

80. Painted Lady
Vanessa cardui
Ventral view

81. Red Admiral
Vanessa atalanta
rubria
Dorsal view

82. Red Admiral
Vanessa atalanta
rubria
Ventral view

83. Buckeye
Junonia coenia
Dorsal view

84. Buckeye
Junonia coenia
Ventral view

85. Red-spotted Purple
*Basilarchia arthemis
astyanax*
Dorsal view

86. Red-spotted Purple
*Basilarchia arthemis
astyanax*
Ventral view

87. Viceroy
Basilarchia archippus
Dorsal view

88. Hackberry Butterfly
Asterocampa celtis
Male dorsal view

89. Tawny Emperor
Asterocampa clyton
Male dorsal view

90. Tawny Emperor
Asterocampa clyton
Female dorsal view

91. Appalachian Eyed
Brown
Satyrodes appalachia
Ventral view

92. Little Wood Satyr
Megisto cymela
Dorsal view

93. Common Wood
   Nymph
Cercyonis pegala
Ventral view

94. Monarch
Danaus plexippus
Female dorsal view

95. Pipe-vine Swallowtail
Battus philenor
Larva

96. Pipe-vine Swallowtail
Battus philenor
Pupa

97. Zebra Swallowtail
Eurytides marcellus
Larva

98. Zebra Swallowtail
Eurytides marcellus
Pupa

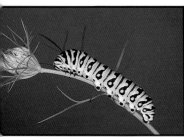

99. Black Swallowtail
Papilio polyxenes asterius
Larva

100. Black Swallowtail
Papilio polyxenes asterius
Pupa

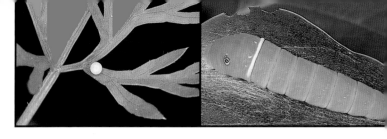

101. Black Swallowtail
Papilio polyxenes asterius
Egg

102. Tiger Swallowtail
Pterourus glaucus
Larva

103. Tiger Swallowtail
Pterourus glaucus
Pupa

104. Spicebush Swallowtail
Pterourus troilus
Larva

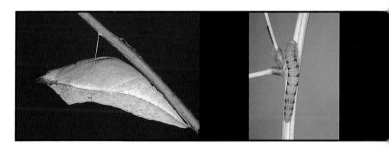

105. Spicebush Swallowtail
Pterourus troilus
Pupa

106. Cloudless Sulphur
Phoebis sennae eubule
Larva

107. Cloudless Sulphur
Phoebis sennae eubule
Pupa

108. Sleepy Orange
Eurema nicippe
Larva

109. Sleepy Orange
Eurema nicippe
Pupa

110. Coral Hairstreak
Harkenclenus titus
Larva

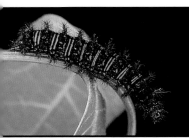

111. Baltimore Checkerspot
Euphydryas phaeton
Larva

112. Question Mark
Polygonia interrogationis
Larva

113. Question Mark
Polygonia interrogationis
Pupa

114. Hop Merchant
Polygonia comma
Larva

115. Hop Merchant
Polygonia comma
Pupa

116. Mourning Cloak
Nymphalis antiopa
Larva

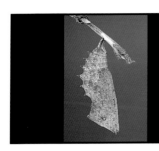

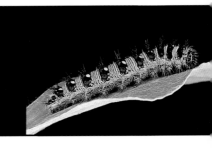

117. Mourning Cloak
Nymphalis antiopa
Pupa

118. American Painted Lady
Vanessa virginiensis
Larva

119. American Painted Lady
Vanessa virginiensis
Pupa

120. Painted Lady
Vanessa cardui
Larva

121. Painted Lady
Vanessa cardui
Pupa

122. Red Admiral
Vanessa atalanta rubria
Larva

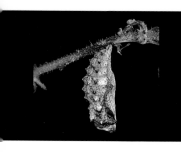

123. Red Admiral
Vanessa atalanta rubria
Pupa

124. Buckeye
Junonia coenia
Larva

125. Buckeye
Junonia coenia
Pupa

126. Viceroy
Basilarchia archippus
Larva

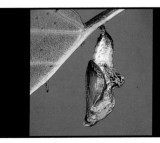

127. Viceroy
Basilarchia archippus
Pupa

128. Hackberry Butterfly
Asterocampa celtis
Larva

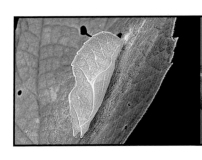

129. Hackberry Butterfly
Asterocampa celtis
Pupa

130. Monarch
Danaus plexippus
Larva

131. Monarch
Danaus plexippus
Pupa

132. Monarch
Danaus plexippus
Egg

HESSEL'S HAIRSTREAK (*Mitoura hesseli*)

Butterfly (Plate 39): This Hairstreak is so similar to the Olive Hairstreak (*Mitoura grynea*) that it was not recognized as a separate species until 1950. Characteristics for separation of the adult butterflies are discussed under the Olive Hairstreak.

Range: The known range of Hessel's Hairstreak extends from southern New Hampshire to the west end of the Florida Panhandle.

Habitat: Hessel's Hairstreak inhabits bogs and swamps where white cedar grows. One can easily overlook it because of its habit of perching high up in white cedar trees.

Adult Food Sources: Nectar is obtained from the flowers of milkweeds, blueberries, chokeberry, dogbane, sweet pepperbush, buttonbush, and sand myrtle.

Immature Stages: The eggs of Hessel's Hairstreak are deposited on white cedar. Larvae and pupae resemble the corresponding stages of the Olive Hairstreak. There are two broods in Delmarva.

BROWN ELFIN (*Incisalia augustinus*)

Butterfly (Plate 40): The upper wing surface of the Brown Elfin is dark brown in the male and reddish brown in the female. The undersurface is medium brown with a darker area toward the wing bases. Prominent spots and lines

---

characteristic of the Eastern Pine Elfin (*Incisalia niphon*) are lacking. The Brown Elfin can be separated from other Elfins occurring in Delmarva by the absence of cloudy gray areas beneath. There are no small tail-like protrusions on the hind wings. The Brown Elfin appears in early spring.

Range: In the east the Brown Elfin ranges from northern Maine south through northern Georgia. In the southern parts of its range, it prefers hilly and mountainous terrain.

Habitat: This Elfin is found in acid bogs, pine and serpentine barrens, and open woodlands.

Adult Food Sources: Blackberry, bearberry, and spicebush serve as nectar sources.

Immature Stages: The blue green eggs are deposited on host inflorescence. Mature caterpillars are green with dorsal and several lateral stripes. They feed on huckleberries and bearberry.

FROSTED ELFIN (*Incisalia irus*)

Butterfly (Plate 41): Males are gray above; females have some light brown areas. They are distinguished from the similar appearing Henry's Elfin (*Incisalia henrici*) by the generally dark brown color below. Henry's Elfin is lighter with a dark basal area and a distinctly lighter outer area on the hind wing.

Range: The Frosted Elfin is found from southern Maine south through Georgia and northern Alabama.

Habitat: This Elfin is usually found in association with its larval food plant, wild indigo, in open woods, along railroad rights-of-way, woodland edges, and roadsides.

Adult Food Sources: Adults are commonly found perched on the larval food plant, but no information is available on adult foods.

Immature Stages: Greenish white eggs are deposited in flower buds and flowers of the host plant. In Delmarva, the usual food of the caterpillar is the flowers and young pods of wild indigo, although lupine may also be utilized. The slug-shaped caterpillars are yellow-green with brown hairs. Differing from most butterflies, pupation occurs in a loose cocoon spun in litter at the base of the food plant.

HENRY'S ELFIN (*Incisalia henrici*)

Butterfly (Plate 42): The appearance of Henry's Elfin differs from that of the similar Frosted Elfin (*Incisalia irus*) by the presence of a dark basal area on the hind wing beneath with an outer contrasting lighter brown area. Henry's can be separated from the Brown Elfin (*Incisalia augustinus*) by the presence of some gray dusting on the ventral hind wing and the presence of short tail-like projections in Henry's Elfin.

Range: The range of Henry's Elfin extends south from Maine to Florida and west to Wisconsin and Texas.

Habitat: Henry's Elfin is found in brushy areas, open roads, pine barrens, wood edges, and powerline cuts.

Adult Food Sources: Blackberries, huckleberry, and redbud are favorite nectar sources.

Immature Stages: Eggs are pale green with white ridges. They are deposited on flowers of the host plant. The caterpillars of this species may be either a dark red-brown with lighter red-brown stripes, or green with lighter green stripes. American holly, redbud, blueberry, and huckleberry are utilized as larval foods.

EASTERN PINE ELFIN (*Incisalia niphon*)

Butterfly (Plate 43): The Eastern Pine Elfin is easily separated from other Elfin species by its strongly banded pattern beneath.

Range: The range of the Eastern Pine Elfin extends from New England westward through the Great Lakes states and south to northern Florida and the Gulf States.

Habitat: Open pine and mixed pine-deciduous woods, woods' edges, and fields with many young pines are favored by the Eastern Pine Elfin.

Adult Food Sources: The Eastern Pine Elfin visits a wide variety of flowers. These include chickweed, dandelion, various cresses, lupine, blueberry, dogbane, milkweeds, and white sweet clover.

Immature Stages: Eggs of this species are pale green. They are laid on new growth of the host plant. Caterpillars are pale green with two whitish lateral stripes and a yellow head. Various species of pines are consumed. Young trees are preferred.

WHITE-M HAIRSTREAK (*Parrhasius m-album*)

Butterfly (Plate 45): The White-M Hairstreak is bright blue with distinct black borders above and gray below, with a distinct white M near the base of the tails. The Delmarva population of this attractive butterfly is variable, but it is seldom abundant.

Range: The range of the White-M Hairstreak extends from the southern border of Massachusetts south to the tip of Florida and west to Kansas and eastern Texas.

Habitat: This butterfly favors open areas and trails in deciduous woods frequently in association with oaks.

Adult Food Sources: The White-M Hairstreak visits milkweeds, sumac, sweet pepperbush, viburnums, and goldenrods.

Immature Stages: The life history of this species is little known, but the eggs are white and presumably laid on the host plant. Caterpillars have green back stripes and seven lateral stripes on a yellow green background. They feed on various species of oaks. There are three generations per year.

GRAY HAIRSTREAK (*Strymon melinus*)

Butterfly (Plate 46): The Gray Hairstreak can be identified by its dark gray upper surface with an orange dot near the base of the tails, and the light gray undersurface, also with an orange dot near the tails. For many years this has been Delmarva's most common species of Hairstreak.

Range: The Gray Hairstreak is found throughout the United States.

Habitat: The Gray Hairstreak occurs in a wide variety of habitats with the exception of deep woods. It is particularly partial to weedy, abandoned fields and other disturbed areas.

Adult Food Sources: Nectar is obtained from a wide variety of flowers. Some favorites are milkweeds, white sweet clover, Canada thistle, dogbane, and goldenrods.

Immature Stages: Pale green eggs are deposited on an inflorescence of the host plant. Caterpillars are variable in color ranging through yellow, green, or brown with lateral stripes. They feed on the leaves, fruit, and flowers of a variety of legumes and mallows. The Gray Hairstreak has three to four broods per year.

Blues: Subfamily Polyommatinae

EASTERN TAILED BLUE (*Everes comyntas*)

Butterfly (Plates 47, 48, 49, and 50): The Eastern Tailed Blue is one of Delmarva's most common species and the only small, tailed butterfly here that is not a Hairstreak. Males are blue above with a black margin. Females are uniformly slate gray above except for those emerging in early spring which have an appreciable amount of blue. Both sexes are smaller than any of the local Hairstreaks.

Range: This species is found throughout the United States east of the Mississippi River with the exception of southern Florida. West of the Mississippi its range extends to central Colorado.

Habitat: The Eastern Tailed Blue favors sunny locations such as open woods, fields, roadsides, and railroad rights-of-way.

Adult Food Sources: Because of its short tongue, the Eastern Tailed Blue is limited to flowers with easily reached nectar. Included are cresses, white clover, white sweet clover, orange milkweed, dogbane, fleabane, and asters.

Immature Stages: The pale green eggs have white longitudinal ridges. They are usually deposited on flowers of the host plant. Caterpillars are dark green with a dark stripe down the middle of the back and faint oblique stripes on the sides. The head is black. The flowers, buds, and leaves of a wide variety of legumes are used as food.

SPRING AZURE (*Celastrina argiolus*)

Butterfly (Plates 51 and 52): This common butterfly is the first to emerge in very early spring. Both sexes are sky blue above; the males with a very narrow black border, and the females with a wide black border. Those emerging in early spring are gray below with black dots and brownish patches. Those emerging later are grayish white below; the dots are faint and the brownish patches absent.

Range: The Spring Azure occurs throughout the United States with the exception of the Florida peninsula.

Habitat: The Spring Azure frequents open deciduous woods, woods' edges, old fields, and wooded swamps.

Adult Food Sources: Favorite nectar sources are spicebush, winter cress, dogbane, milkweeds, and New Jersey tea.

Immature Stages: Eggs of this species are pale green with white ridges. They are deposited on young leaves or inflorescence of the host plant. Mature caterpillars are pink or greenish yellow with a dark stripe down the back and greenish stripes on the sides. They feed on the flowers and buds of a wide variety of trees and shrubs, including flowering dogwood and other species of dogwood, New Jersey tea, meadowsweet, staghorn sumac, black snakeroot, and blueberries. There are four to five broods per year.

Snout Butterflies
Family Libytheidae

Members of this small family are characterized by very elongated labial palpi. Various species of hackberry are the only larval food plants. On Delmarva there is but one representative, the Snout Butterfly. It is medium sized with a forewing length of 1.1 to 1.4 centimeters.

SNOUT BUTTERFLY (*Libytheana bachmanii*)

Butterfly (Plate 53): The "proboscis" or "snout" (elongated labial palpi) of the Snout Butterfly sets it apart from all other eastern butterflies. The dorsal wing pattern of large orange-brown spots on a dark brown background plus white spots on the forewing is distinctive. The hind wing below can be either a uniform gray or mottled black and brown.

Range: The breeding range of the Snout Butterfly extends from the southeastern corner of Virginia southward through the Carolinas, Georgia, Florida, the Gulf States, west Texas, Arizona, and southern California. From the Gulf States, the breeding range extends north to southern Illinois. In the warm months the Snout greatly extends its range northward through emigration, but it cannot survive the winter north of the breeding range.

Habitat: Open woods, road edges, wooded river bottoms, and bushy fields are utilized.

Adult Food Sources: Adults visit sweet pepperbush, goldenrods, dogbane, dogwood, and many other flowers.

Immature Stages: Pale green eggs are deposited on young leaves or leaf petioles. Mature caterpillars are green with a yellow strip on the back and two along the sides. Just back of the head there is a hump with two black tubercles. Hackberry is the only larval food. The chrysalis is green and tapered at both ends. The number of broods is uncertain.

Brushfoots
Family Nymphalidae

This is the largest family of the true butterflies. All members of this family have small forelegs that are useless for walking but have numerous receptors for the detection of odors. There is a wide size range of the forewing from 1.4 to 4.8 centimeters.

The caterpillars of this family are diverse in appearance. Many have longitudinal rows of tubercles on the body and "horns" or "antlers" on the head; others are relatively smooth. Pupae also vary in appearance, but like all Nymphalidae, they are suspended with the head end downward.

Adults of many members of this family prefer to feed on tree sap, aphid honeydew, fermenting fruit, or dung, and visit flowers infrequently. Some prefer nectar.

Fritillaries: Subfamily Argynninae

VARIEGATED FRITILLARY (*Euptoieta claudia*)

Butterfly (Plate 55): "Variegated" is an apt description of this medium-sized butterfly with its confused pattern of black dots and lines on a reddish brown background. Although the markings on the upper side of the wings are somewhat similar to those of the Great Spangled Fritillary (*Speyeria cybele*), the absence of ventral silver spots easily separates it from that species.

Range: The breeding range of this species is confined to the coastal areas of the Carolinas, Georgia, the Gulf States, and all of Florida. In the summer it commonly emigrates to the north as far as southern Canada. Immigrants frequently establish temporary colonies, but they cannot survive the winter in Delmarva. The butterfly can be seen in Delmarva from late April until frost, but it is most common in August and September.

Habitat: The Variegated Fritillary prefers open fields, meadows, and roadsides.

Adult Food Sources: This Fritillary is particularly fond of various milkweeds, dogbane, and knapweeds.

Immature Stages: Eggs are pale green or yellowish. They are deposited on leaves of the host plant. The mature caterpillar is red orange with two lateral stripes of mixed black and white spots. There are also six rows of black spines, the front pair being the longest. The head is red. A variety of unrelated plant species serve as food for the larvae. These include passionflower, violets, May apple, and purslane.

The chrysalis is pearly white with numerous small black and orange dots. There are usually three broods per year in Delmarva.

GREAT SPANGLED FRITILLARY (*Speyeria cybele*)

Butterfly (Plates 56 and 57): The Great Spangled Fritillary is a large orange-brown butterfly with silver spots on the underside of the hind wings. There is no other common butterfly with these markings in Delmarva. Males emerge one to three weeks earlier than females. The sexes are similar in appearance.

Range: The Great Spangled Fritillary ranges throughout the eastern United States as far south as the northern parts of Georgia and the Gulf States. To the west it extends to the Pacific Coast.

Habitat: This butterfly likes meadows, open fields, and roadsides where the larval food plants, violets, are found. However, it is a strong flier and may be found anywhere suitable nectar sources are available.

Adult Food Sources: Various species of milkweeds, thistles, ironweeds, Joe-Pye-weed, bergamot, and dogbane are visited.

Immature Stages: Eggs are deposited in late summer and hatch in the fall. Caterpillars of the Great Spangled Fritillary feed on various species of violets. The tiny larvae do not start to feed until spring and then only at night. When mature, the caterpillars are black with many black spines that are orange at the base.

REGAL FRITILLARY (*Speyeria idalia*)

Butterfly (Plates 58 and 59): This species is easily distinguished from other eastern fritillaries by the iridescent deep blue of the hind wings above, plus two parallel rows of spots, both white in the female and one white and one orange brown in the male. Males emerge one to three weeks before females.

Range: In the eastern United States, the Regal Fritillary is found from Maine to North Carolina, primarily in piedmont and mountain areas. The range extends in a broad band westward to Colorado.

Habitat: In the eastern part of its range, the Regal Fritillary inhabits wet meadows, marshy areas, and nearby open fields. It generally occurs in small local colonies. This beautiful butterfly was once fairly common, but in recent years colonies have been rapidly disappearing due to habitat destruction.

Adult Food Sources: Milkweeds and thistles are preferred by the Regal Fritillary.

Immature Stages: Eggs are deposited in the fall but not always on the food plants, violets. After hatching in late fall, the young caterpillars hibernate and do not begin feeding until spring. Fully grown larvae are black, mottled with dull yellow or orange. There are many spines, white with black tips along the back, and with orange bases on the sides.

SILVER-BORDERED FRITILLARY (*Clossiana selene*)

Butterfly (Plates 60 and 61): The color and pattern of the upper surface of the wings of both the Silver-bordered and the Meadow Fritillary (*Clossiana bellona*) are generally similar to that of the Great Spangled Fritillary (*Speyeria cybele*), but the wing expanse is only one-half that of the Great Spangled. The underside of the Silver-bordered Fritillary has many silvery spots that are absent from the Meadow Fritillary.

Range: The Silver-bordered Fritillary is a northern species with a range extending from northern New England to northern Delaware and Maryland. It is also found in the mountains of Virginia and West Virginia and as far west as Illinois.

Habitat: The Silver-bordered Fritillary frequents swamps, bogs, wet meadows, and other wet or damp areas.

Adult Food Sources: Various milkweeds and thistles are preferred by the Silver-bordered Fritillary.

Immature Stages: The pale green or yellowish eggs are laid near, but not on, the food plant. Caterpillars are greenish brown, mottled with darker patches. Numerous spines are present, the first pair much longer than the others. Various species of violets are utilized as food. There are three broods per year.

MEADOW FRITILLARY (*Clossiana bellona*)

Butterfly (Plates 62 and 63): The Meadow Fritillary is much more common than the Silver-bordered Fritillary (*Clossiana selene*). For distinguishing features, refer to the discussion under the Silver-bordered Fritillary.

Range: In the eastern United States, the range of the Meadow Fritillary extends from Nova Scotia south to western North Carolina and the eastern tip of Tennessee, and west through the states bordering the Great Lakes.

Habitat: Wet or damp meadows and open fields are the usual habitats for the Meadow Fritillary.

Adult Food Sources: Verbenas, dogbane, dandelion, and black-eyed Susan are frequent choices of this butterfly.

Immature Stages: Eggs are deposited at random near, but not on, violets. Mature larvae are purplish black with irregular yellow spots and brown spines. The caterpillar food plants are various species of violet. There are three broods per year.

Checkerspots: Subfamily Melitaeinae

SILVERY CHECKERSPOT (*Charidryas nycteis*)

Butterfly (Plates 64 and 65): The upper wing surfaces of both the Silvery Checkerspot and the look-alike Pearl Crescent (*Phyciodes tharos*) are orange brown marked with black. These black markings are clear-cut in the Silvery

Checkerspot and slightly blurred in the Pearl Crescent. A less subjective characteristic differentiating the two is the broad off-white band that crosses the ventral hind wing of the Silvery Checkerspot.

Range: The Silvery Checkerspot ranges from Maine to northern Delaware, western Maryland, western Virginia, the Carolinas, and the northern halves of the Gulf States. To the west it extends to Texas and Montana.

Habitat: The Silvery Checkerspot frequents damp, partially open areas, usually near water.

Adult Food Sources: Many species of flowers serve as sources of nectar. Among them are various milkweeds, dogbane, red clover, and thin-leaved sunflower.

Immature Stages: Clusters of greenish eggs are deposited on the undersides of the host plant leaves. Young caterpillars feed together in a group and winter as immature caterpillars which resume feeding and growth in the spring. Mature caterpillars are black with a dull orange stripe, white speckles, and black spines. The chrysalis varies in color from white with brown mottling to green, brown, or gray.

In Delmarva, the Silvery Checkerspot is frequently associated with the thin-leaved sunflower, but other wild sunflowers and wingstem also serve as food. There are two broods annually.

PEARL CRESCENT (*Phyciodes tharos*)

Butterfly (Plates 66 and 67): One of our most common species of small butterflies, the Pearl Crescent resembles a small Silvery Checkerspot (*Charidryas nycteis*). The Pearl Crescent can be distinguished from the Checkerspot by the less sharply defined black areas above and the absence of a broad whitish band on the underside of the hind wing.

Range: The Pearl Crescent ranges from central New England to the tip of Florida and west to Montana, Texas, and Mexico.

Habitat: This species is found in many types of open habitat including meadows, fields, roadsides, and railroad rights-of-way.

Adult Food Sources: The Pearl Crescent has been observed gathering nectar at over thirty flower species. These include milkweeds, dogbane, asters, black-eyed Susan, and white clover.

Immature Stages: Clusters of pale green eggs are laid on the underside of food plant leaves. Newly hatched larvae feed in groups and hibernate during the winter before they are fully grown. Growth resumes in the spring. Mature larvae are chocolate brown with a yellowish stripe along each side. There are also numerous yellowish spines.

The larval food consists of various species of asters. The chrysalis is gray or brown. The Pearl Crescent reproduces continuously as long as there is sufficient food and temperatures remain suitable.

BALTIMORE CHECKERSPOT (*Euphydryas phaeton*)

Butterfly (Plate 68): The distinctive black and orange wing pattern of the Baltimore is a warning to predators that it is both unpalatable and emetic.

Range: The Baltimore is found from the Maritime Provinces of Canada to northern Georgia and westward to the eastern border of the Dakotas and Oklahoma.

Habitat: In Delmarva, the butterfly is found in wet meadows, usually in association with its food plants.

Adult Food Sources: Flowers are visited infrequently, but adults sometimes seek nectar in wild roses, milkweeds, and Canada thistle.

Immature Stages (Plate 111): The female deposits large masses of yellow eggs on the food plants: turtlehead, English plantain, and hairy beardtongue. The young caterpillars feed together in a web until late fall. At this time they leave their food plants and hibernate in the ground litter. When spring arrives, the larvae may continue to feed on their original food plant, or they may wander and complete development on a wide variety of unrelated species.

Mature caterpillars are striped transversely with alternate orange and black. There are several rows of branched black spines. The chrysalis is white with many orange and black spots. There is only one brood per year.

Anglewings: Subfamily Nymphalinae

QUESTION MARK (*Polygonia interrogationis*)

Butterfly (Plates 69, 70, and 71): The Question Mark is larger than the Hop Merchant (*Polygonia comma*); otherwise, the two species are quite similar in appearance.

In both species the irregular wing outline and the mottled brown and light brown ventral wing markings closely resemble a dead leaf. A silvery comma-shaped mark at the center of the hind wing below distinguishes the Hop Merchant. The Question Mark has a similar mark plus a dot. Each species has a summer form in which the basal half of the hind wing above is solid black, and a fall form in which this area is orange brown with dark dots and blotches. The hind wings of both species are edged with a dusting of blue violet, particularly in the fall form.

Range: The Question Mark is found from southern Maine to central Florida and west to the Rocky Mountains.

Habitat: The Question Mark frequents open woods, particularly along the edges of woodland roads and trails. Winters are passed in hibernation within hollow logs and trees, under loose shingles, and in woodpiles.

Adult Food Sources: Adults of the Question Mark prefer to feed on aphid honeydew, tree sap, fermenting fruit, or animal dung. If foods of this nature are not available, they will obtain nectar from milkweeds, sweet pepperbush, and other flowers.

Immature Stages (Plates 112 and 113): Pale green eggs are deposited singly or in groups, usually on plants near the host but not on it. The basic color of mature caterpillars varies from black to yellow with yellow or red longitudinal lines. There are several spines and tubercles; these may be yellow, red orange, or black. Caterpillars feed on stinging and false nettles, American and slippery elm, and hackberry. Pupae are yellow or dark brown with silvery spots. There are two generations per year.

HOP MERCHANT (*Polygonia comma*)

Butterfly (Plates 72, 73, and 74): Although it is very similar to the Question Mark (*Polygonia interrogationis*), the Hop Merchant is slightly smaller and has a silvery comma on the underside of its hind wing instead of a question mark. For additional information on identification, refer to the discussion under the Question Mark.

Range: The Hop Merchant, also known as the Comma, inhabits an area extending from southern Canada south to the northern halves of South Carolina, Georgia, and the Gulf States. To the west its range includes Iowa, Kansas, and Nebraska.

Habitat: The Hop Merchant frequents open woods, woodland roads, trail edges, moist fields, and disturbed areas.

Adult Food Sources: Like the Question Mark, the Hop Merchant prefers fermenting fruit, tree sap, aphid honeydew, and animal droppings to floral nectar.

Immature Stages (Plates 114 and 115): The pale green eggs are deposited on the undersides of leaves of the food plant. Caterpillars vary from brown to greenish brown and whitish with numerous dark or white spines. The chrysalis is brown or gray with silver and gold protuberances on the abdomen.

   The larvae feed on stinging nettle, false nettle, and American elm. There are two generations per year.

MOURNING CLOAK (*Nymphalis antiopa*)

Butterfly (Plate 75): The Mourning Cloak is easily identified by the yellow band and row of blue dots on the wing edges. The dark underside provides concealment when the butterfly is perching on the bark of trees with its wings folded. The sexes are similar in appearance. Mourning Cloaks overwinter in the adult stage and may live as long as ten months. They frequently emerge temporarily from hibernation during warm winter days in February and March when they may be observed along sunny paths and in woodland clearings. During periods of hot summer weather, they estivate in hollow trees and other shelters.

Range: The Mourning Cloak occurs throughout Canada and the United States with the exception of the arctic regions and Florida.

Habitat: Adult Mourning Cloaks frequent open deciduous woods and suburban areas.

Adult Food Sources: This species prefers tree sap and fermenting fruit to floral nectar. Flowers of milkweeds, dogbane, and New Jersey tea are visited occasionally.

Immature Stages (Plates 116 and 117): Eggs are deposited in clusters on twigs of the host plants of American elm, hackberry, and various willow species. The caterpillars are black, speckled with tiny white dots. The prolegs are orange red and the back has conspicuous red dots and blackish spines.

The chrysalis is gray or brown with two short "horns" on the head and pointed tubercles along the back. There is usually only one generation per year.

AMERICAN PAINTED LADY (*Vanessa virginiensis*)

Butterfly (Plates 77 and 78): The American Painted Lady and the Painted Lady (*Vanessa cardui*) are similar in general appearance. They can be differentiated by the number of distinct eyespots on the underside of the hind wing: two for the American Painted Lady and five for the Painted Lady.

Range: The American Painted Lady inhabits the entire United States, southern Canada, Mexico, and northern South America.

Habitat: This butterfly favors open fields, meadows, gardens, and disturbed areas.

Adult Food Sources: American Painted Lady nectars at a wide variety of flowers. These include dogbane, goldenrods, ironweeds, milkweeds, sweet pepperbush, thistles, buttonbush, and zinnias.

Immature Stages (Plates 118 and 119): Eggs are laid on plantain-leaved pussytoes or everlasting. Larvae live individually in a nest constructed of silk and the leaves of the food plant. Caterpillar feeding damage is easily recognized by the uneaten remnants of the leaf's white woolly surface layer.

Mature caterpillars are black with groups of threadlike, alternating, transverse yellow and black bands. Between these bands are white and orange-red dots. The chrysalis is either green or greenish with darker markings. There are two broods per year.

PAINTED LADY (*Vanessa cardui*)

Butterfly (Plates 79 and 80) This relative of the American Painted Lady (*Vanessa virginiensis*) is also called the Thistle Butterfly. In general, it resembles the American Painted Lady but has five prominent eyespots on the ventral side of the hind wing instead of two.

Range: The Painted Lady is the world's most widely distributed butterfly, occurring throughout north America (except for the far northern regions), Central America, Africa, the West Indies, and many other areas. Populations north of the Gulf States cannot survive harsh winters and are replaced by emigrants from the south, which recolonize fields and open places.

Habitat: The Painted Lady is usually found in fields, gardens, and disturbed areas.

Adult Food Sources: Thistles, ironweeds, Joe-Pye-weed, milkweeds, sweet pepperbush, buttonbush, red clover, and many other flowers are visited for food.

Immature Stages (Plates 120 and 121): Pale green eggs are deposited on the upper surface of the host plant leaf. A great many plant species are used as larval food; the most favored are thistles, common mallow, and hollyhock.

The caterpillar is yellow green, mottled with black, and has a yellow lateral stripe. The chrysalis is gray or gold with several projections. The number of broods varies from one to four a year.

RED ADMIRAL (*Vanessa atalanta rubria*)

Butterfly (Plates 81 and 82): The wings of the Red Admiral are distinguished by a dark upper surface with a transverse band of orange red across the forewing and along the edge of the hind wing.

Range: The range of the Red Admiral includes all of North America with the exception of the far north. It also is found in Europe, North Africa, and Asia Minor.

Habitat: One of the earliest butterflies to appear in the spring, adults prefer woodlands and open areas. Males utilize sunny perches on woodland edges to intercept females.

Adult Food Sources: Red Admirals prefer tree sap, fermenting fruit, and bird droppings to flower nectar. If these foods are not available, they will visit milkweeds, dogbane, red clover, and sweet pepperbush.

Immature Stages (Plates 122 and 123): Pale green eggs are laid on the upper surface of host plants. Larvae of the Red Admiral vary in color from black to yellow green. Black and yellow lateral stripes and branched spines are also present. They live in shelters constructed from leaves of the host plants—stinging nettle and wood nettle. The pupa is brown with gold dorsal tubercles. There are two broods annually.

BUCKEYE (*Junonia coenia*)

Butterfly (Plates 83 and 84): With a total of six large eyespots above, the Buckeye cannot be mistaken for any other Delmarva butterfly. Individuals emerging in the summer are primarily tan beneath, while those emerging in the fall are pinkish or reddish.

Range: The Buckeye occurs throughout most of the United States, but it can survive the winter

---

only in Florida and the coastal areas of the Carolinas, Georgia, and the Gulf States. The colder areas of its range are repopulated annually by emigrants, the first arriving in Delmarva in late April.

Habitat: Adult Buckeyes can be found in open areas with low vegetation and in bare areas such as dry fields, beach dunes, railroad rights-of-way, and powerline cuts.

Adult Food Sources: Buckeyes seek nectar from many flowers including goldenrods, knapweeds, dogbane, tickseed sunflower, and asters. Along the Delmarva coast, seaside goldenrod is a particular favorite.

Immature Stages (Plates 124 and 125): Food plants include purple gerardia, false foxglove, plantain, and ruellias. In Delmarva purple gerardia is a favorite host plant. Buckeye caterpillars are black with lateral and dorsal yellow lines and tiny blue dots. Four rows of spines are present. The pupa is dull white, mottled with dark gray and black. There are two or three generations annually.

Admirals: Subfamily Limenitidinae

RED-SPOTTED PURPLE (*Basilarchia arthemis astyanax*)

Butterfly (Plates 85 and 86): The species *Basilarchia arthemis* is divided into two subspecies. Except for possible strays only *Basilarchia arthemis astyanax* has been found

---

in Delmarva. Subspecies *astyanax* is black above with a large area of bright blue on the hind wing. Ventrally the color is bluish black with several large orange spots including a row along the edge of the hind wing. Except for the absence of tails, *astyanax* is an excellent mimic of the distasteful and toxic Pipe-vine Swallowtail *(Battus philenor)*. The subspecies *B. a. arthemis* (White Admiral) is similar to *B. a. astyanax* except for the addition of a broad white band that crosses both wings above and below.

Range: The Red-spotted Purple is found throughout the United States east of the Rocky Mountains, except southern Florida and central Texas. To the north its range extends from the Canadian Maritime Provinces to central Alaska. The White Admiral is found in the northern parts of the range (southern New England, New York, in the mountains of Pennsylvania and Maryland, and in Michigan and Minnesota). Interbreeding occurs in areas where the ranges overlap.

Habitat: The Red-spotted Purple inhabits woodlands where it favors woods' edges, paths, and trails.

Adult Food Sources: Fermenting fruit, tree sap, dead animals, and dung are the usual food sources of the Red-spotted Purple. On rare occasions, the small white flowers of Hercules' club, sweet pepperbush, and white species of the genus *Eupatorium* (for example, bonesets, thoroughworts, and Joe-Pye-weeds) are visited. In Delmarva, the butterfly has been observed gathering nectar at hyssop-leaved boneset.

Immature Stages: Greenish gray eggs are laid individually on leaves of the host plant. Larvae of the Red-Spotted Purple feed on the leaves of wild cherry, poplars, aspens, and some oaks.

Colored a mixture of olive green, black, and white, the caterpillars closely resemble bird droppings. A pair of antennalike protuberances are located just behind the head. The chrysalis is a mixture of brown, gray, and white with a prominent disc-shaped bulge at the base of the abdomen. There are two to three broods per year.

VICEROY (*Basilarchia archippus*)

Butterfly (Plate 87): The orange red background and black veining of the Viceroy closely resemble the colors and markings of the Monarch (*Danaus plexippus*). The best distinguishing feature is a black line which crosses the hind wing of the Viceroy but is absent in the Monarch. Long thought to be a classic example of an edible species mimicking a distasteful one (the Monarch), it has recently been demonstrated that the Viceroy is also distasteful. See the discussion under Mimicry, page 18.

Range: The Viceroy occurs throughout the eastern United States and westward almost to the Pacific Coast.

Habitat: The Viceroy is found in or near open wet or damp areas such as swamps, marshes, and the edges of ponds and streams.

Adult Food Sources: Early season individuals prefer carrion, animal dung, tree sap, and aphid honeydew to flowers. Later in the year they seek the nectar of Joy-Pye-weed, asters, goldenrods, and other aster family members.

Immature Stages (Plates 126 and 127): Pale green or yellow eggs are deposited on the upper surface of host plant leaves. The caterpillar and chrysalis of the Viceroy resemble those of the Red-spotted Purple (*Basilarchia arthemis astyanax*) very closely. Viceroy caterpillars feed on willows and poplars. There are three broods annually.

Hackberry And Goatweed Butterflies
Family Apaturidae

This family includes two subfamilies, Apaturinae, Hackberry Butterflies, and Charaxinae, Goatweed Butterflies. Members of the genus *Asterocampa* are the only representatives of the family Apaturidae occurring in Delmarva. Apaturidae are medium-sized butterflies with forewing lengths ranging from 2.2 to 3.4 centimeters. They are rapid-flying, active butterflies that prefer rotten fruit, tree sap, and dung to nectar. Their larvae feed only on hackberry.

Hackberry Butterflies: Subfamily Apaturinae

HACKBERRY BUTTERFLY (*Asterocampa celtis*)

Butterfly (Plate 88): The Hackberry Butterfly, also known as the Gray Emperor, is a rapid flier which frequently perches in the sun on the leaves or trunk of hackberry, the larval food plant. Also, they often alight on a warm would-be collector or photographer and drink from the droplets of perspiration on the surprised individual.

The Hackberry Butterfly is easily distinguished from the Tawny Emperor (*Asterocampa clyton*) by the presence of an eyespot and white markings on the forewing above, which are absent in the Tawny Emperor. Females have larger and broader wings than the males.

Range: The range of the Hackberry Butterfly extends from southern New England south to the tip of Florida, and west to include Minnesota and Arizona.

Habitat: This species frequents wooded stream and river edges and forest openings, usually associated with the larval food plants, hackberry trees.

Adult Food Sources: The Hackberry Butterfly seldom visits flowers, preferring rotten fruit, aphid honeydew, tree sap, dead animals, and dung.

Immature Stages (Plate 128 and 129): The white eggs are deposited in clusters on the food plant. Caterpillars have longitudinal yellow stripes on a green background. The head bears two forked "antlers," and the posterior end is forked. The pupa is green with faint yellow lines and a pair of short horns on the anterior end. Hackberry is the only food plant. There are two broods per year.

TAWNY EMPEROR (*Asterocampa clyton*)

Butterfly (Plates 89 and 90): The Tawny Emperor is larger than the Hackberry Butterfly (*Asterocampa celtis*) and lacks the eyespot and white marks of the forewing above. The wings of the female are larger, more rounded, than those of males.

Range: The range of the Tawny Emperor extends from southern New York State south to Florida and west to Colorado and eastern Texas.

Habitat: The Tawny Emperor frequents open woodlands and forests' edges, often in association with hackberry trees and the Hackberry Butterfly.

Adult Food Sources: The Tawny Emperor likes rotten or fermenting fruit, aphid honeydew, tree sap, dead animals, and animal dung.

Immature Stages: White eggs are laid in clusters on the food plant. Caterpillars can be distinguished from those of the Hackberry Butterfly by the presence of a narrow blue stripe down the center of the back. The chrysalis is almost identical to that of the Hackberry Butterfly. There are two broods annually.

Browns, Satyrs, and Wood Nymphs
Family Satyridae

Butterflies of the family Satyridae are gray or brownish with prominent eyespots on the undersides of the hind wings. They are medium

sized with forewing lengths ranging from 1.8 to
3.2 centimeters.

They frequent woods, woods' edges, and
wet areas. Flowers are seldom visited since tree
sap, fermenting fruit, or dung are preferred
foods. Larvae consume grasses and sedges.

Browns: Subfamily Elymniinae

APPALACHIAN EYED BROWN (*Satyrodes
appalachia*)

Butterfly (Plate 91): The ventral surface is tan
with darker brown wavy lines. There are
marginal rows of six eyespots on the hind wing
and four on the forewing. These serve to
distinguish the Appalachian Eyed Brown from
the Little Wood Satyr (*Megisto cymela*), which
has only two large eyespots on the ventral side
of each wing.

In 1970 the Appalachian Eyed Brown was
first recognized as a separate species, having
previously been confused with the Eyed Brown
(*Satyrodes eurydice*). The latter species does not
occur in Delmarva.

Range: The range of the Appalachian Eyed
Brown is not confined to the Appalachians but
includes central New England to southern
South Carolina, the northern parts of the Gulf
States, northern Florida, Tennessee, and
southern Kentucky. It also extends west into
Wisconsin. North of Delaware its range overlaps
with that of the Eyed Brown, a closely related
species.

Habitat: The Appalachian Eyed Brown favors wet woodlands, swamps and bogs, and wet meadows adjacent to woods.

Adult Food Sources: Tree sap is the only known food of the Appalachian Eyed Brown.

Immature Stages: Caterpillars are green with yellow lengthwise stripes and two red hornlike projections on the head. The chrysalis is green. Sedge is the only larval food reported in the northeast. There is one brood per year.

Satyrs and Wood Nymphs: Subfamily Satyrinae

LITTLE WOOD SATYR (*Megisto cymela*)

Butterfly (Plate 92): This common butterfly is easily recognized by the pair of large black-centered yellow eyespots that occur in each wing, both above and below.

Range: Except for northern Maine and southern Florida, the Little Wood Satyr is found throughout the eastern United States. It extends westward to the eastern edge of Montana and then south along the eastern edge of Nebraska and Texas.

Habitat: The Little Wood Satyr frequents woods and woods' edges.

Adult Food Sources: Aphid honeydew and tree sap are the main adult foods. Occasional visits are made to common milkweed, white sweet clover, and staghorn sumac.

Immature Stages: Pale yellow green eggs are laid in or near grass. The caterpillars are greenish brown with fine hairs, lengthwise stripes, and whitish tubercles. They feed on orchard grass and other grasses. The chrysalis is green. There is a single generation each year.

COMMON WOOD NYMPH (*Cercyonis pegala*)

Butterfly (Plate 93): The appearance of this butterfly differs considerably in different parts of its range. In Delmarva it is distinguished by a large orange-yellow forewing patch with two large eyespots.

Range: The Common Wood Nymph occurs in the entire eastern United States with the exception of northern Maine and southern Florida.

Habitat: This butterfly likes open woods, damp meadows, and bogs.

Adult Food Sources: Major sources of food are rotting fruit and occasionally nectar from ironweeds, fleabane, and sunflowers.

Immature Stages: Yellow eggs are laid in or near grasses. They do not hatch until the following spring. Caterpillars of the Common Wood Nymph are yellow green with four lighter yellow, lengthwise stripes, and a red fork at the posterior end. The chrysalis is green and plump. There is a single brood per year.

Milkweed Butterflies
Family Danaidae
Subfamily Danainae

Most members of this family live in tropical or subtropical regions. The principal larval food is various species of milkweed. Cardiac glycosides in the food plant make both larva and adult toxic and emetic to predators. The only species in Delmarva is the Monarch. It is a large butterfly with a forewing length of 4.3 to 5.9 centimeters.

MONARCH (*Danaus plexippus*)

Butterfly (Plate 94): The Monarch is distinguished by wings of reddish orange with black veining, black wing markings, and white spots. It is closely mimicked by the Viceroy (*Basilarchia archippus*). The most distinguishing feature is the black line that crosses the hind wing of the Viceroy. This is absent in the Monarch. The male can be distinguished from the female by the presence of a small black scent patch on a hind wing vein.

While most adult Monarchs are distasteful and toxic to birds, the degree depends on the amount of the toxic compounds present in the caterpillar's host plant. This can vary between milkweed species and between populations of a species.

Range: The Monarch occurs from southern
Canada throughout the United States into
Mexico and Central America.

Migration: The two-way annual mass migration
of the Monarch is unique. No other North
American butterfly migrates south in the fall
and north in the spring. Some of the eastern
population of Monarchs winter along the
southern Atlantic Coast, the Gulf Coast of
Florida, and some Caribbean islands, but the
majority fly to a relatively small area in the
Mexican uplands. It is here, in early spring, that
most mating takes place before the return
migration starts.

Only a very few individuals complete the
long return journey to the northern parts of
their range. Most stop at some intermediate
point where the female deposits her eggs. Their
progeny in turn mate, fly further north, and
repeat the process. This continues until the
entire Monarch range is repopulated.

Habitat: The Monarch frequents fields,
roadsides, meadows, gardens, and other areas,
particularly where milkweeds are present.

Adult Food Sources: Monarchs visit a wide
variety of plants for nectar. Favorites include
milkweeds, ironweeds, Joe-Pye-weed,
goldenrods, buttonbush, red clover, sweet
pepperbush, dogbane, and thistles.

Immature Stages (Plates 130, 131, and 132):
Eggs are white, somewhat conical, with ribs and
pits. They are glued to the undersides of leaves
of the food plant. Newly hatched larvae must

consume the eggshell or die. The caterpillar is white with transverse, narrow, yellow and black stripes. The chrysalis is stout, rounded, and green with gold dots.

In Delmarva Monarch larvae feed almost exclusively on various milkweeds, although the caterpillars are occasionally found on dogbane.

Stray Species

Note: In addition to the butterflies included in the Species Accounts, which are either year-round residents of the Delmarva Peninsula or immigrants usually present in appreciable numbers, there are reliable reports of the rare occurrence of the following seven additional species.

Family Papilionidae
Subfamily Papilioninae

GIANT SWALLOWTAIL (*Heraclides cresphontes*)

(Plate 7): The Giant Swallowtail is the largest of the Swallowtails seen in Delmarva with a forewing length of 4.6 to 7.4 centimeters. Below, it is mostly yellow, and above, black with one wide yellow band across the forewings and another that parallels the outer edges of both hind wings. It is found throughout the southern states where its larvae are sometimes a minor pest on citrus. Further north it occurs as a casual stray or in local colonies where the larvae feed on northern prickly ash, southern prickly

ash, or Hercules' club, and hop tree. None of these food plants is widespread on the Delmarva Peninsula, and there are no records of the occurrence of breeding populations.

Family Pieridae
Subfamily Pierinae

GREAT SOUTHERN WHITE (*Ascia monuste phileta*)

The Great Southern White is a rare immigrant from the south. Larger than the Cabbage Butterfly (*Pieris rapae*), it is white above with a series of small black triangles on the outer edge of the forewing in the male and on both the forewings and hind wing in the female. The forewing length ranges from 2.7 to 3.9 centimeters.

Family Lycaenidae
Subfamily Theclinae

NORTHERN HAIRSTREAK (*Fixsenia ontario*)

Plate 44: This rare Hairstreak might be confused with the common Gray Hairstreak (*Strymon melinus*). In Delmarva specimens the ground color of the underside of the wings of the Gray Hairstreak is gray, while that of the Northern Hairstreak is brown. The M-shaped mark on the underside of the hind wing and the black and white line extending from it have an orange component that is lacking in the Northern Hairstreak.

Family Heliconiidae
Subfamily Heliconiinae

GULF FRITILLARY (*Agraulis vanillae*)

Plate 54: With many silvery spots below and
orange brown with black lines and spots above,
the color pattern of the Gulf Fritillary resembles
that of many species of the genus *Speyeria*.
These are represented on Delmarva by the
Great Spangled *(Speyeria cybele)* and Regal
Fritillaries *(S. idalia)*. However, the Gulf
Fritillary's elongated, narrow wing shape is
distinctive. Forewing length varies from 3.1 to
4.5 centimeters.

   Because the Gulf Fritillary is known to
migrate, individuals reported from Delmarva
are probably immigrants; but since a larval food
plant, maypops (passionflower) occurs in
southern Delmarva, temporary breeding
populations are possible.

Family Nymphalidae
Subfamily Nymphalinae

GRAY COMMA (*Polygonia progne*)

In size, form, and color, the Gray Comma
resembles the Hop Merchant (*Polygonia
comma*). The outer dark band on the upper side
of the hind wings is more distinct and the dots
within the band much smaller than in the Hop
Merchant. Beneath, the Gray Comma has a
large, dark gray area with a lighter gray area
toward the wing edges; the small silvery mark
on the hind wing is shaped like an L rather than
a comma.

COMPTON TORTOISE SHELL (*Nymphalis vaualbum*)

The Compton Tortoise Shell wings resemble those of the Mourning Cloak (*Nymphalis antiopa*) in size and shape. The undersides of the wings are mottled gray and brown with a small white V in the center of each hind wing. The upper wings are a rich mixture of brownish yellow and large black spots. Each wing also has a single white spot.

Compton Tortoise Shell is a northern species that has occasional population explosions. It is assumed that reports of this species in Delmarva are the result of immigration from normal source areas during periods of high numbers.

MILBERT'S TORTOISE SHELL (*Aglais milberti*)

(Plate 76): Milbert's Tortoise Shell is a northern species resembling the Hop Merchant (*Polygonia comma*) in size and wing shape. The broad orange and yellow band which crosses the upper side of both wings is distinctive.

III. ENJOYING BUTTERFLIES

Butterflies and Gardens

Butterfly gardens are becoming popular across the country as awareness of the need to protect butterflies and their habitats grows. Butterflies are crucial to the environment as effective pollinators of crops and flowers, sensitive indicators of ecological health, and major links in the food chain (especially as larvae). Gardens play an important part in ensuring their survival because they can provide much-needed food and areas for mating and resting.

Not only will butterflies flitting gently about the garden add to its natural beauty, but they will also provide an opportunity for people to become acquainted with the various species, their life histories, and their behavior. Males of some species may be observed as they establish the territories they defend against other butterflies, insects, and sometimes humans. Although mating procedures may only rarely be observed, there are few pleasures that equal the delight of seeing butterflies basking in the sunlight of a garden.

Modification of existing gardens to make them more attractive to adult butterflies usually requires the introduction of good nectar sources throughout the growing season. Butterflies are influenced in their selection of these nectar sources by abundance, color, ease of obtaining nectar, and height of the plant. Nectar-feeding butterflies prefer flower species with many accessible nectar sources grouped closely together, such as butterfly bush, milkweeds, and various members of the aster family.

Flower size is also important, as the small, short-tongued species of Lepidoptera cannot reach the nectar of large flowers. Odor and color, too, can influence the butterfly's choice of flower. But of all the factors contributing to the selection of the nectar sources, availability is the most important. Thus, in early spring, when blossoms are scarce, Delmarva Swallowtail butterflies frequently feed on dandelion flowers. Later in the season, when many other flowers are available, dandelions are largely ignored.

Butterflies have good color vision. Most favor white, yellow, orange, pink, or purple flowers. A few are attracted to red or blue. However, since butterflies have vision in the ultraviolet range of the spectrum, their perception of the appearance of flowers may differ from that of humans.

Table 2 shows some wild and domestic plants that are suitable for butterfly gardens on the Delmarva Peninsula. To avoid damage to natural populations of native plants, only those species available as seeds or plants from nurseries should be used.

Table 2. Some Preferred Nectar Sources

DOMESTIC

ageratum
bergamot
buddleia (white, purple, or lilac varieties)
clovers
coreopsis
cosmos
cultivars of native *Eupatorium* species
daisies
gardenia
heliotrope
lantana
lilac
lobelia
marigold
petunia
phlox
red clover
scabiosa
sweet clover
zinnia

WILD

asters
bergamot
black-eyed Susan
boneset
butterfly weed
buttonbush
cardinal flower
chokeberry (red and black)
cut-leaved toothwort
dandelion
dogbane

Continued on next page

Table 2—*Continued*

field chickweed
goldenrods
ironweed
Joe-Pye-weed
knapweeds
lilies (Turks'-cap, tiger, cultivars of native species)
purple loosestrife
milkweeds (common, orange, purple, swamp)
mistflower
mountain mint
New Jersey tea
blue phlox
pussy willow
sassafras
sweet pepperbush
thistles
tickseed sunflower (and other *Bidens* species)

Several Delmarva butterflies favor nonfloral foods such as animal dung, carrion, bird droppings, fermenting fruit, aphid honeydew, and tree sap. Most of these butterflies visit flowers only when they are unable to locate their preferred foods. They can be attracted by painting tree trunks with a fermenting mixture composed of kitchen odds and ends such as spoiled fruit or fruit juices, molasses, brown sugar, beer, and yeast. This is best done at a distance from the house, as flies and hornets may also visit. Attractive feeding stations utilizing sugar solutions are available commercially.

In addition to flowers, shrubs, and small trees, patches of bare ground and rocks are used by many species of butterflies for sunbathing, resting, or watching for possible mates. Puddles or damp spots where minerals are being leached from the soil are favorite gathering places for the males of Swallowtails and several other species. Apparently, male butterflies require more sodium than do females, and often congregate in these areas for that reason.

For additional information on gardening for butterflies see the References and Additional Reading section.

Photographing Butterflies

If you would enjoy having a visual record of the various butterflies you have seen, photography can provide you with full-color, accurate likenesses that are long-lasting and much easier to care for than a collection of pinned specimens. Photos require a comparatively small storage space, and there will be no problem with dermestid beetles or other destructive insects. Photography also can record the colors and physical apprearance of eggs, larvae, and pupae.

A single lens reflex (SLR) camera body is a necessity for photographing butterflies, but it need not be a recent model. Many older manually operated cameras are capable of taking excellent photographs, provided compatible lenses and an electronic flash are available.

The lens is the most critical element in obtaining photographs sharp enough for satisfactory enlargement. For closeup work specially corrected lenses, usually termed macro or micro, are necessary. They are available from several manufacturers to fit most makes of camera bodies, and come in 50 mm, 55 mm,

60 mm, 90 mm, 100 mm, and 105 mm focal lengths. The 50 mm-60 mm lenses are excellent for photographing stationary subjects such as insect eggs, larvae, and pupae; but the distance between the subject and the lens will be so small that it will be difficult to closely approach living butterflies without alarming them. Lenses with focal lengths of 90 mm-105 mm provide a longer and more usable working distance. At the closest focusing distance, a macro lens should have a subject:image ratio of 1:1; that is, the image on the film will be the same size as the subject. (A ratio of 1:2 indicates an image size $\frac{1}{2}$ that of the subject; 1:4 an image size of $\frac{1}{4}$, etc. Image size at various distances is usually marked on the lens barrel.) It should be possible with this lens to use increasingly smaller ratios (1:10) and finally to infinity.

In closeup photography good depth of field is required for the subject to be uniformly sharp. To achieve this image, small apertures (large-numbered f stops) must be used. Therefore, a macro lens should be capable of stopping down to f/16, and many can be stopped down to f/22 or f/32.

The photographer has a choice between slide (reversal) film and print film, and within these categories, between fast and relatively slow film. In both kinds, the slower films (ISO 25-100) are less expensive than the fast films (ISO 200-1000). In general, the slower films give a sharper image and better color rendition, although fast films have been measurably improved recently. Correct exposure is critical for slide film since errors in exposure cannot be corrected during development as they can be with print film.

Because of the need to use small apertures in closeup photography, the natural light available may present problems in obtaining adequate exposure. If a tripod can be used, the correct exposure can usually be obtained with a slow shutter speed. However, few butterflies will remain posed long enough for a tripod to be set up and adjusted. Therefore, most outdoor photography is done with the camera hand held using shutter speeds of $\frac{1}{60}$ second or faster for acceptably sharp photographs. For maximum sharpness and clarity when hand holding the camera, use high-speed films of ISO 400-1000.

In order to use low-speed films successfully, it frequently is necessary to augment the natural light by using an electronic flash that is synchronized with the camera shutter. The synchronization speed should be $\frac{1}{60}$ second or faster for hand-held work.

A multitude of electronic flashes are available. For closeup photography with low-speed film (ISO 25-100) a Guide Number (GN) of 80-90 should be adequate. GN equals flash-to-subject distance in feet × f stop. Distance is sometimes expressed in meters. To convert a GN from meters to feet, divide by 3.27. A provision for reducing the power of the flash is a very useful feature of some models.

APPENDIX A: Plant List

Note: This list includes the common and scientific names of food plants referred to in the text by common name only.

ageratum—*Eupatorium* spp.
alders—*Alnus* spp.
alfalfa—*Medicago sativa*
American elm—*Ulmus americana*
American holly—*Ilex opaca*
apple—*Malus pumila*
ashes—*Fraxinus* spp.
aspens—*Populus* spp.
aster family—Asteraceae
Atlantic white cedar—*Chamaecyparis thyoides*
azaleas—*Rhododendron* spp.
bearberry—*Arctostaphylos uva-ursi*
beeches—*Fagus* spp.
bergamot—*Monarda fistulosa*
black snakeroot—*Cimicifuga racemosa*
black walnut—*Juglans nigra*
blackberry—*Rubus* spp.
black-eyed Susan—*Rudbeckia hirta*
blue flag—*Iris versicolor*
blueberries—*Vaccinium* spp.
boneset—*Eupatorium perfoliatum*

broccoli—*Brassica oleracea broccoli*
Brussels sprouts—*Brassica oleracea gemmifera*
butterfly bush—*Buddleia* spp.
butterfly weed—*Asclepias tuberosa*
butternut—*Juglans cinerea*
buttonbush—*Cephalanthus occidentalis*
Canada thistle—*Cirsium arvense*
cardinal flowers—*Lobelia cardinalis*
carrots—*Daucus* spp.
cauliflower—*Brassica oleracea botrytis*
celery—*Apium graveolens*
chickweeds—*Stellaria* spp. or *Cerastium* spp.
chokeberries—*Aronia* spp.
  black—*A. melanocarpa*
  red—*A. arbutifolia*
clovers—*Trifolium* spp., *Melilotus* spp. or
  Lespedeza spp.
common mallow—*Malva neglecta*
coreopsis—*Coreopsis* spp.
cosmos—*Cosmos* spp.
cresses—*Arabis* spp., *Cardamine* spp., or
  Barbarea spp.
curled dock—*Rumex crispus*
cut-leaved toothwort—*Dentaria laciniata*
daisies—*Chrysanthemum* spp.
dame's rocket—*Hesperis matronalis*
dandelion—*Taraxacum officinale*
dill—*Anethum graveolens*
dogbanes—*Apocynum* spp.
dogwood, flowering—*Cornus florida*
dogwoods—*Cornus* spp.
dutchman's pipe—*Aristolochia durior*
English plantain—*Plantago lanceolata*
eupatoriums—*Eupatorium* spp.
everlasting—*Graphalium obtusifolium*
fall asters—*Aster* spp.
false foxglove—*Aureolaria virginica*

---

false nettle—*Boehmeria cylindrica*
field chickweed—*Cerastium arvense*
fleabanes—*Erigeron* spp.
goldenrods—*Solidago* spp.
grasses—members of family Gramineae
groundsel tree—*Baccharis halimifolia*
hackberry—*Celtis occidentalis*
hairy beardtongue—*Penstemon hirsutus*
heliotropes—*Heliotropium* spp.
Hercules' club—*Zanthoxylum clava-herculis*
hollyhocks—*Althea* spp.
hop tree—*Ptelea trifoliata*
horse-sugar—*Symplocos tinctoria*
huckleberries—*Gaylussacia* spp.
hyssop-leaved boneset—*Eupatorium
        hyssopifolium*
ironweeds—*Vernonia* spp.
Japanese honeysuckle—*Lonicera japonica*
Joe-Pye-weed (common)—*Eupatorium dubium*
knapweeds—*Centaurea* spp.
lantanas—*Lantana* spp.
legumes—Leguminosae
lilacs—*Syringa vulgaris* or *S. persica*
lobelias—*Lobelia* spp.
lupine—*Lupinus perennis*
mallows—Malvaceae
marigolds—*Tagetes* spp.
May apple—*Podophyllum peltatum*
maypops—*Passiflora incarnata*
meadowsweet—*Spiraea latifolia*
milkweeds—*Asclepias* spp.
        common—*A. syriaca*
        orange—*A. lanceolata*
        purple—*A. purpurascens*
        swamp—*A. incarnata*
mint family—Labiatae
mistflower—*Eupatorium coelestinum*

mistletoe—*Phoradendron flavescens*
morning glories—*Ipomoea* spp.
mountain mints—*Pycnanthemum* spp.
mustard family—Cruciferae
nasturtiums—*Tropaeolum* spp.
New Jersey tea—*Ceanothus americanus*
New York ironweed—*Vernonia noveboracensis*
northern prickly ash—*Zanthoxylum americanium*
oaks—*Quercus* spp.
orchard grass—*Dactylis glomerata*
parsley family—Umbelliferae
parsley—*Pastinaca sativa*
parsnip—*Thaspium barbinode*
partridge pea—*Cassia fasciculata*
passionflower or maypops—*Passiflora incarnata*
pawpaw—*Asimina triloba*
peppergrass—*Lepidium virginicum*
petunias—*Petunia* spp.
phlox—*Phlox* spp.
     blue—*P. divaricata*
pine family—Pinaceae
pines—*Pinus* spp.
plantains—*Plantago* spp.
plantain-leaved pussytoes—*Antennaria
     plantaginifolia*
poplars—*Populus* spp.
purple gerardia—*Gerardia purpurea*
purple loosestrife—*Lythrum salicaria*
purslane—*Portulaca oleracea*
pussy willow—*Salix discolor*
pussytoes—*Antennaria* spp.
red bay—*Persea borbonia*
red cedar—*Juniperus virginiana*
red clover—*Trifolium pratense*
redbud—*Cercis canadensis*
ruellias—*Ruellia* spp.
sand myrtle—*Leiophyllum buxifolium*

sassafras—*Sassafras albidum*
scabiosas—*Scabiosa* spp.
seaside goldenrod—*Solidago sempervirens*
sedges—members of family Cyperaceae
senna—*Cassia hebicarpa*
sensitive plant—*Cassia nictitans*
shadbush—*Amelanchier canadensis*
sheep sorrel—*Rumex acetosella*
shepherd's purse—*Capsella bursa-pastoris*
slippery elm—*Ulmus rubra*
sourwood—*Oxydendron arboreum*
southern prickly ash or Hercules'
      club—*Zanthoxylum clava-herculis*
spicebush—*Lindera benzoin*
stinging nettles—*Urtica dioica*
sumac—*Rhus* spp.
      dwarf—*R. copallina*
      staghorn—*R. typhina*
sunflowers—*Helianthus* spp.
sweet bay—*Magnolia virginiana*
sweet clovers—*Melilotus* spp.
sweet pepperbush—*Clethra alnifolia*
sweetleaf—*Symplocos tinctoria*
thin-leaved sunflower—*Helianthus decapetalus*
thistles—*Cirsium* spp.
thoroughworts—*Eupatorium* spp.
tickseed sunflower—*Bidens polylepis*
tiger lily—*Lilium tigrinum*
tulip poplar—*Liriodendron tulipifera*
Turk's-cap lily—*Lilium superbum*
turtlehead—*Chelone glabra*
verbenas—*Verbena* spp.
vetches—*Vicia* spp.
viburnums—*Viburnum* spp.
violets—*Viola* spp.
Virginia snakeroot—*Aristolochia serpentaria*
walnut, black—*Juglans nigra*

water dock—*Rumex orbiculatus*
watercress—*Nasturtium officinale*
wax myrtle—*Myrica cerifera*
white cedar—*Chamaecyparis thyoides*
white clover—*Trifolium repens*
white sweet clover—*Melilotus alba*
wild carrot—*Daucus carota*
wild cherry—*Prunus serotina*
wild ginger—*Asarum canadense*
wild indigo—*Baptisia tinctoria*
wild morning glory—*Ipomoea purpurea*
wild mustard—*Brassica* spp.
wild plum—*Prunus americana* or
    P. angustifolia
wild roses—*Rosa* spp.
wild strawberry—*Fragaria virginiana*
wild sunflowers—*Helianthus* spp.
willows—*Salix* spp.
wingstem—*Actinomeris alternifolia*
winter cress—*Barbarea verna*
witch hazel—*Hamamelis virginiana*
wood nettle—*Laportea canadensis*
yarrow—*Achillea millefolium*
zinnia—*Zinnia elegans*

APPENDIX B: Butterfly Checklist

Swallowtails
Family Papilionidae
Subfamily Papilioninae

Pipe-vine Swallowtail (*Battus philenor*)
Zebra Swallowtail (*Eurytides marcellus*)
Black Swallowtail (*Papilio polyxenes asterius*)
Tiger Swallowtail (*Pterourus glaucus*)
Spicebush Swallowtail (*Pterourus troilus*)
Palamedes Swallowtail (*Pterourus palamedes*)

Whites, Orange Tips, and Sulphurs
Family Pieridae

Whites
Subfamily Pierinae

Checkered White (*Pontia protodice*)
Cabbage Butterfly (*Pieris rapae*)

Orange Tips
Subfamily Anthocharinae

Falcate Orange Tip (*Paramidia midea*)

Sulphurs
Subfamily Coliadinae

Clouded Sulphur (*Colias philodice*)
Alfalfa Butterfly (*Colias eurytheme*)
Cloudless Sulphur (*Phoebis sennae ebule*)
Little Sulphur (*Eurema lisa*)
Sleepy Orange (*Eurema nicippe*)

Gossamer Wings
Family Lycaenidae

Harvesters
Subfamily Miletinae

Harvester (*Feniseca tarquinius*)

Coppers
Subfamily Lycaeninae

Little Copper (*Lycaena phlaeas*)
Bronze Copper (*Hyllolycaena hyllus*)

Hairstreaks and Elfins
Subfamily Theclinae

Great Purple Hairstreak (*Atlides halesus*)
Coral Hairstreak (*Harkenclenus titus*)
Banded Hairstreak (*Satyrium calanus*)
King's Hairstreak (*Satyrium kingi*)
Striped Hairstreak (*Satyrium liparops*)
Red-banded Hairstreak (*Calycopis cecrops*)
Olive Hairstreak (*Mitoura grynea*)
Hessel's Hairstreak (*Mitoura hesseli*)
Brown Elfin (*Incisalia augustinus*)

Frosted Elfin (*Incisalia irus*)
Henry's Elfin (*Incisalia henrici*)
Eastern Pine Elfin (*Incisalia niphon*)
White-M Hairstreak (*Parrhasius m-album*)
Gray Hairstreak (*Strymon melinus*)

Blues
Subfamily Polyommatinae

Eastern Tailed Blue (*Everes comyntas*)
Spring Azure (*Celastrina argiolus*)

Snout Butterflies
Family Libytheidae

Snout Butterfly (*Libytheana bachmanii*)

Brushfoots
Family Nymphalidae
Fritillaries
Subfamily Argynninae

Variegated Fritillary (*Euptoieta claudia*)
Great Spangled Fritillary (*Speyeria cybele*)
Regal Fritillary (*Speyeria idalia*)
Silver-bordered Fritillary (*Clossiana selene*)
Meadow Fritillary (*Clossiana bellona*)

Checkerspots
Subfamily Melitaeinae

Silvery Checkerspot (*Charidryas nycteis*)
Pearl Crescent (*Phyciodes tharos*)
Baltimore Checkerspot (*Euphydryas phaeton*)

Anglewings
Subfamily Nymphalinae

Question Mark (*Polygonia interrogationis*)
Hop Merchant (*Polygonia comma*)
Mourning Cloak (*Nymphalis antiopa*)
American Painted Lady (*Vanessa virginiensis*)
Painted Lady (*Vanessa cardui*)
Red Admiral (*Vanessa atalanta rubria*)
Buckeye (*Junonia coenia*)

Admirals
Subfamily Limenitidinae

Red-spotted Purple (*Basilarchia arthemis astyanax*)
Viceroy (*Basilarchia archippus*)

Family Apaturidae
Hackberry Butterflies
Subfamily Apaturinae

Hackberry Butterfly (*Asterocampa celtis*)
Tawny Emperor (*Asterocampa clyton*)

Family Satyridae
Browns
Subfamily Elymniinae

Appalachian Eyed Brown (*Satyrodes appalachia*)

Satyrs and Wood Nymphs
Subfamily Satyrinae

Little Wood Satyr (*Megisto cymela*)
Common Wood Nymph (*Cercyonis pegala*)

Milkweed Butterflies
Family Danaidae, Subfamily Danainae

Monarch (*Danaus plexippus*)

Stray Species

Giant Swallowtail (*Heraclides cresphontes*)
Great Southern White (*Ascia monuste phileta*)
Northern Hairstreak (*Fixsenia ontario*)
Gulf Fritillary (*Agraulis vanillae*)
Gray Comma (*Polygonia progne*)
Compton Tortoise Shell (*Nymphalis vaualbum*)
Milbert's Tortoise Shell (*Aglais milberti*)

REFERENCES AND ADDITIONAL READING

Chevron Chemical Company, The. 1991. *How to attract hummingbirds and butterflies*. An Ortho Book. Lithographed by Webcrafters, Inc.

Comstock, J. H. 1933. *An introduction to entomology*. Ithaca, NY: Comstock Publishing Co., Inc.

Covell, C. V. 1977. Check list of the butterflies and skippers of Virginia. *Virginia Journal of Science* 18/1:21-24.

Fales, J. H. 1974. Check list of the skippers and butterflies of Maryland. *Chesapeake Science* 15/4:222-29.

Fales, J. H. and W. R. Grooms. 1980. Notes on butterfly collecting in Maryland in 1979. *Maryland Entomologist* 1/4:12-13.

Holland, W. J. 1991. *The butterfly book*. Revised Edition. Garden City, NY: Doubleday, Doran and Company, Inc.

Howe, W. H. 1975. *The butterflies of North America*. Garden City: NY: Doubleday and Company, Inc.

Klots, A. B. 1951. *A field guide to the butterflies of North America, east of the Great Plains*. Peterson Field Guide Series. Boston, MA: Houghton Mifflin Co.

Miller, J. 1992. *Common names of North American butterflies*. Washington, DC: Smithsonian Institution Press.

Opler, P. A. and G. O. Krizek. 1984. *Butterflies east of the Great Plains*. Baltimore, MD: The Johns Hopkins University Press.

Pyle, R. M. 1981. *The Audubon Society field guide to North American butterflies*. Chanticleer Press Edition. New York, NY: Alfred A. Knopf.

Ritland, D. B. and L. P. Brower. 1991. The viceroy butterfly is not a batesian mimic. *Nature* 350/63218:497-98.

Scott, J. A. 1986. *The butterflies of North America*. Stanford, CA: Stanford University Press.

Shapiro, A. M. 1951. *Butterflies of the Delaware Valley*. Special Publication of the American Entomological Society. Ann Arbor, MI: Cushing-Malloy, Inc.

Simmons, R. S. 1956. Notes on ten new butterfly records for the state of Maryland. *The Lepidopterist News* 10/5:157-59.

Simmons, R. S. and W. A. Anderson. 1970 (1971). Eighteen new or scarce butterflies from the state of Maryland. *Journal of Research on the Lepidoptera* 9/3:175-84.

Stokes, D. and L., and E. Williams. 1991. *The butterfly book: An easy guide to butterfly gardening, identification, and behavior*. Boston, MA: Little, Brown and Company.

Tatnall, R. R. 1946. *The flora of Delaware and the Eastern Shore*. Society of Natural

History of Delaware. Lancaster, PA:
Intelligences Printing Co.

Tekulsky, M. 1985. *The butterfly garden*. Boston,
MA: The Harvard Common Press.

Tietz, H. M. 1952. *Lepidoptera of Pennsylvania*.
State College, PA: Pennsylvania School of
Agriculture.

Wickler, W. 1968. *Mimicry in plants and
animals*. World University Library. New
York, NY: McGraw Hill Book Company.

Xerces Society, The, in association with The
Smithsonian Institution. 1990. *Butterfly
gardening: Creating summer magic in
your garden*. San Francisco, CA: Sierra
Club Books in association with the
National Wildlife Federation.

INDEX OF BUTTERFLIES

Bracketed numbers indicate the first page of each species account and boldface numbers indicate plate numbers.

B

C

Cloudless Sulphur, 5, 29, [45], 46, 112, **Pls. 24, 106, 107**

Coliadinae, 44, 112

Colias eurytheme, 23, 28, 40, [44], 47, 112, **Pls. 22, 23**

Colias philodice, 28, 40, [44], 112, **Pl. 21**

color, 16, 17

Common Wood Nymph, 16, 27, 29, [92], 115, **Pl. 93**

Compton Tortoise Shell, 5, [98], 116

Coppers, 7, 48, 51, 113

Coral Hairstreak, [53], 113, **Pls. 34, 110**

D

Danaidae, 6, 7, 93, 115

Danainae, 6, 93, 115

Danaus plexippus, 17, 23, 26, 29, 86, [93], 115, **Pls. 94, 130, 131, 132**

Delmarva peninsula, 4

disturbed areas, 27

dunes, 26

E

Eastern Pine Elfin, 27, 60, [62], 113, **Pl. 43**

Eastern Tailed Blue, 49, [64], 113, **Pls. 94, 130, 131, 132**

eggs, 18, 30

Elfins, 48, 49, 53, 113

Elymniinae, 90, 115

enemies, 23

Epargyreus clarus, 8

Euphydryas phaeton, 28, [76], 114, **Pls. 68, 111**

Euptoieta claudia, 26, 29, [68], 114, **Pl. 55**

Eurema lisa, 29, [46], 112, **Pl. 25**

Eurema nicippe, 29, [47], 112, **Pls. 26, 108, 109**

Eurytides marcellus, 26, 27, [33], 36, 112, **Pls. 3, 97, 98**

Everes comyntas, [64], 113, **Pls. 47, 48, 49, 50**

Eyed Brown, 90

eyes, 11, 20

Hessel's Hairstreak, 27, 58, [59], 113, **Pl. 39**

Hop Merchant, 16, 23, 27, 30, 77, [78], 97, 98, 114,
   Pls. 72, 73, 74, 114, 115

Hyllolycaena hyllus, 28, [52], 113, **Pls. 30, 31, 32**

Hymenoptera, 23

I

Incisalia augustinus, 27, [59], 61, 113, **Pl. 40**

Incisalia henrici, 27, 60, [61], 113, **Pl. 42**

Incisalia irus 27, [60], 61, 113, **Pl. 41**

Incisalia niphon, 27, 60, [62], 113, **Pl. 43**

Insecta, 9

instar, 20

J

Junonia coenia, 5, 26, 29, [83], 115, **Pls. 83, 84, 124, 125**

K

King's Hairstreak, [55], 113

L

larva, 19,

legs, 14, 20

Lepidoptera, 9, 18

Libytheana bachmanii, [67], 114, **Pl. 53**

Libytheidae, 6, 7, 66, 114

life cycle, 18

life span, 23

Limenitidinae, 84, 115

Little Copper, [51], 113, **Pls. 28, 29**

Little Sulphur, 29, [46], 112, **Pl. 25**

Little Wood Satyr, 16, 27, 29, 90, [91], 115, **Pl. 92**

Lycaena phlaeas, [51], 113, **Pls. 28, 29**

Lycaenidae, 6, 7, 48, 49, 96, 113

Lycaeninae, 48, 51, 113

INDEX OF PLANTS

boneset, 28, 85, 101
broccoli, 42
Brussels sprouts, 42
buddleia, 101
butterfly bush, 32, 35, 37, 42, 100
butterfly weed, 101
butternut leaves, 55
buttonbush, 37, 59, 81, 82, 94, 101

C

cabbage, 42
Canada thistle, 64, 76
cardinal flowers, 46, 101
carrots, 35
cauliflower, 42
celery, 35
chickweed, 43, 62
chokeberry, 57, 59, 101
clover, 44, 101
common mallow, 82
coreopsis, 101
cosmos, 101
cresses, 41, 43, 62, 65
curled dock, 48, 52
cut-leaved toothwort, 43, 101

D

daisies, 101
dame's rocket, 33
dandelions, 34, 38, 42, 43, 44, 62, 73, 100, 101
dill, 35
dogbane, 34, 38, 54, 55, 56, 57, 58, 59, 62, 64, 65, 66, 67, 69, 70, 73, 74, 75, 80, 81, 83, 84, 94, 95, 101
dogwood, 66, 67
dutchman's pipe, 33
dwarf sumacs, 58

K
knapweeds, 69, 84, 102

L
lantana, 46, 101
legumes, 40, 64, 65
lilacs, 32, 34, 37, 102
lilies, 102
lobelia, 101
lupine, 61, 62

M
mallows, 64
marigold, 101
May apple, 69
maypops, 97
meadowsweet, 55, 66
milkweeds, 28, 32, 34, 35, 36, 38, 41, 44, 51, 52, 54, 55, 56, 57, 58, 59, 62, 63, 64, 66, 69, 70, 71, 72, 74, 75, 76, 78, 79, 80, 81, 82, 83, 92, 93, 94, 95, 100, 102
mint family, 42
mistflower, 26, 28, 102
mistletoe, 53
morning glories, 46
mountain mint, 102
mustard family 40, 41, 42, 43
mustards, 41, 42, 43

N
nasturtiums, 42
New Jersey tea, 54, 55, 56, 57, 66, 80, 102
New York ironweed, 35
northern prickly ash, 95

O
oak, 55, 58, 63, 86

W

watercress, 41, 42

water dock, 48, 52

wax myrtle, 58

white cedar, 29, 59

white clover, 45, 51, 65, 75

white sweet clover, 45, 54, 55, 56, 58, 62, 64, 65, 92

wild carrot, 35

wild cherry, 37, 54, 57, 86

wild ginger, 33

wild morning glories, 46

wild mustards, 42

wild plum, 54, 57

wild roses, 76

wild strawberry, 43

wild sunflowers, 74

willow, 28, 80

wingstem, 74

winter cress, 43, 58, 66

witch hazel, 50

wood nettle, 83

Y

yarrow, 51, 55

Z

zinnia, 35, 81, 101

ABOUT THE DELAWARE
NATURE SOCIETY

A nonprofit membership organization, the Delaware Nature Society was founded in 1964 with a mission to foster understanding, appreciation, and enjoyment of the natural world through education, to preserve ecologically significant areas, and to advocate stewardship and conservation of natural resources. Two nature centers, Ashland near Hockessin, Delaware, and Abbott's Mill near Milford, offer a wealth of year-round educational programs for all ages.

The Delaware Nature Society conducts research and publishes books on natural history topics, and undertook *Butterflies of Delmarva* in order to call attention to the beauty and diversity of butterflies local to the region. By appealing to amateur naturalists, gardeners, and landowners, the society seeks to heighten their awareness of the value of native species and the need to protect habitat and preserve natural areas.

For more information about programs, services, and natural history topics, please contact the Delaware Nature Society, P.O. Box 700, Hockessin, DE 19707, or phone (302) 239-2334.